Anarcho-Syndicalism

Rudolf Rocker

PREFACE BY NOAM CHOMSKY

INTRODUCTION BY NICOLAS WALTER

Pluto Press

LONDON • STERLING, VIRGINIA

First published 1989 by Pluto Press
345 Archway Road, London N6 5AA
and 22883 Quicksilver Drive, Sterling, VA 20166-2012, USA

www.plutobooks.com

British Library Cataloguing in Publication Data
A catalogue record for this book is available from the British
Library

Library of Congress Cataloging in Publication Data
Applied for

ISBN   0 7453 1392 2 hardback
ISBN   0 7453 1387 6 paperback

Printed and bound by CPI Group (UK) Ltd, Croydon, CR0 4YY

Contents

Preface

NOAM CHOMSKY

The publication of Rudolf Rocker's *Anarcho-Syndicalism*, after far
too many years, is an event of much importance for people who
are concerned with problems of liberty and justice. Speaking
personally, I became acquainted with Rocker's publications in the
early years of the Second World War, in anarchist book stores and
offices in New York City, and came upon the present work on the
dusty shelves of a university library, unknown and unread, a few
years later. I found it an inspiration then, and have turned back to
it many times in the years since. I felt at once, and still feel, that
Rocker was pointing the way to a much better world, one that is
within our grasp, one that may well be the only alternative to the
'universal catastrophe' towards which 'we are driving on under full
sail', as he saw on the eve of the Second World War. This
catastrophe will be beyond the limits he could then imagine, as
states have acquired the capacity to obliterate human society, a
capacity that they will exercise if the current social order evolves
along its present paths.

Rocker's vision stands in opposition to all of the dominant
tendencies in modern social and political thought. As he recognised
and explained with great clarity, all of these tendencies destroy 'the
impulse to self-help, by inoculating people with the ruinous
delusion that salvation always comes from above', not from their
own conscious understanding and constructive work in 'creating the
living germs of *the new society*', in Bakunin's words. Dominant
currents, understandably enough, aim at subordination of the public.
It is unnecessary to dwell on the so-called 'socialist' states or the
Marxist-Leninist movements. Within the industrial democracies, a
similar conception is firmly rooted among elite groups, whatever
their political persuasion, and is often quite clearly articulated. The
role of the public is to ratify decisions taken elsewhere, to adopt the
doctrines prepared for them by their superiors, and in general to
observe passively while performing their duty. Not all would express

this understanding with the clarity of Juan Bravo Murillo, whom Rocker quotes (p. 118), but his words in fact capture prevailing elite conceptions, accurately if crudely.

In Rocker's radically different conception, people must take their lives and their work into their own hands. Only through their own struggle for liberation will ordinary people come to comprehend their true nature, suppressed and distorted within institutional structures designed to assure obedience and subordination. Only in this way will people develop more humane ethical standards, 'a new sense of right', 'the consciousness of their strength and their importance as a social factor in the life of their time' and of their capacity to realise the strivings of their 'inmost nature'. Such direct engagement in the work of social reconstruction is a prerequisite for coming to perceive this 'inmost nature' and is the indispensable foundation upon which it can flourish.

Rocker surveys the development of these ideas and the struggle to achieve them, and illuminates their fundamental significance. His approach is far from 'utopian'; this is not an abstract discourse, but a guide to action, drawing from the lessons of past failures and successes. Like other serious anarchists, Rocker 'rejects all absolute schemes and concepts' and appreciates that we can set no 'definite final goals for human development', but can only contemplate 'an unlimited perfectibility of social arrangements and human living conditions, which are always straining after higher forms of expression', based on new understanding, new insight. The lessons of history teach us a good deal, but nothing more clearly than the fact that we often remain quite unaware of the forms of oppression of which we are victims, or sometimes agents, until social struggle liberates our consciousness and understanding.

Rocker expresses throughout his faith in the capacity of ordinary people to construct for themselves a world suited to their inner needs, to create and participate in an advancing culture of liberation in free communities, to discover through their own thought and engagement the institutional arrangements that can best satisfy their deeply rooted striving for freedom, justice, compassion and solidarity, at a particular historical moment. This vision remains as inspiring as when it was written a half century ago, and no less valid as a stimulus to our thinking and our constructive action.

Cambridge, Mass.

Introduction
NICOLAS WALTER

Rudolf Rocker (1873–1958) was born in Mainz, in the German Rhineland, into a Catholic family of skilled workers with liberal views. His parents died young, and he was sent to a Catholic orphanage. He was apprenticed as a bookbinder, and followed the trade as a travelling journeyman for several years. He became a socialist in his youth, and joined the Social Democratic Party; but he supported the left-wing opposition group of Die Jungen (The Young), was expelled in 1890, and soon moved towards anarchism. He visited several parts of Western Europe, following his trade and his political interests. He observed the second congress of the Second International in Brussels in 1891, began contributing to the anarchist press in 1892, and left Germany to escape police harassment in 1892. He lived for a couple of years in Paris, and then settled permanently in Britain in 1895.

Although Rocker was a Gentile, he became involved in the Jewish anarchist movement. He learnt Yiddish, lived in the Jewish community, and became the lifelong companion of Milly Witcop (1877–1953). He quickly became a prominent speaker and writer, on cultural as well as political topics, and for 20 years he was the most liked and respected person in the movement. In 1898 he edited *Dos Fraye Vort* (The Free Word), a new Yiddish weekly paper in Liverpool, for a couple of months, and then became editor of *Der Arbeter Fraint* (The Workers' Friend), a revived Yiddish weekly paper in London, and in 1900 also of *Germinal*, a new Yiddish monthly.

The Jewish anarchist movement became larger than the native movement in Britain. A federation of Jewish anarchist groups was formed in 1902, the circulation of the papers and other publications increased, and a thriving social club was opened in Jubilee Street in East London in 1906. Rocker was the most influential figure in the movement, representing it at the International Anarchist Congress in Amsterdam in 1907, and becoming a member of the International Anarchist Bureau established there. The Jewish anarchists were very active in the growing trade union movement, and Rocker favoured the development of anarcho-syndicalism as a new form of anarchist theory and practice.

In 1914 Rocker vigorously opposed both sides in the First World War, and after a few months he was interned as an enemy alien. Soon afterwards the *Arbeter Fraint* was suppressed and the Jubilee Street club closed. The Jewish anarchist movement in Britain never really recovered, and most of its members were later attracted to Zionism or Communism.

In 1918 Rocker was deported from Britain to the Netherlands, and soon after he returned to his native country, Germany. He become a leading figure in the German and indeed the international anarcho-syndicalist movement. He was an active member of the Freie Vereinigung Deutscher Gewerkschaften (Free Association of German Trade Unions) and then a main founder of the Freie Arbeiter-Union Deutschlands (Free Workers' Union of Germany) and editor of its paper, *Der Syndikalist*. He was the moving spirit of the International Congress in Berlin in 1922 which led to the formation of the International Working Men's Association, and acted as one of its secretaries. He used his influence to oppose anarchist support for the Bolshevik Revolution after 1917 or for Peter Arshinov's *Organisational Platform* (which advocated reforming the anarchist movement as a virtual political party) after 1926, and he led the libertarian opposition to the rising Nazi movement.

In 1933 Rocker had to leave Germany again to escape persecution by the new Nazi regime. He settled in the United States, which he had previously visited for lecture tours, and he continued to work as a speaker and writer, directing his efforts against the twin evils of Fascism and Communism. He spent the last 20 years of his life as a leading figure in the Mohegan community at Crompond, New York, and was the best-known anarchist in the country until his death. He supported the Allies in the Second World War, which caused a breach with some old comrades, but he continued to receive more admiration and affection than any veteran of the movement since Kropotkin or Malatesta.

Rocker was a prolific speaker and writer in both Yiddish and German, and he produced a great many articles and pamphlets and several books – especially a libertarian study of the conflict between nationalism and culture, biographies of the anarchist leaders Johann Most and Max Nettlau, and a long autobiography. Many of his writings were translated into Spanish and widely circulated in Latin America, but not many appeared in English. Apart from a few pamphlets, three books were published in the United States – the ambitious study of *Nationalism and Culture* (1937), an essay in literary criticism called *The Six* (1938) and a popular survey of *Pioneers of American Freedom* (1949). Two more were published in Britain – a popular survey of *Anarcho-Syndicalism* (1938), and the section of his autobiography covering *The London Years* (1956). Some others were translated into English but not published – especially *Behind Barbed Wire and Bars*, an account of his internment during the First World War.

The most accessible of Rocker's books is *Anarcho-Syndicalism*. This arose from the Civil War and Revolution in Spain, which broke out in 1936 and brought anarchism and syndicalism back on to the political stage for the first time since the First World War and the Russian Revolution. It was also in 1936 that Fredric Warburg took over the publishing business of Martin Secker and made the new company of Secker & Warburg one of the main London publishers. He specialised in good fiction, especially by leading foreign writers, and in political books by unorthodox writers, whom he described in the second volume of his memoirs, *All Authors are Equal* (1973), as 'a miscellaneous collection of socialists, anarchists, radicals, independent socialists ... pacifists and eccentrics', and among whom were several who later contributed to the anarchist press (such as Jomo Kenyatta, Ethel Mannin, George Orwell, Reginald Reynolds and F. A. Ridley). He took a particular interest in Spain, commenting in the first volume of his memoirs, *An Occupation for Gentlemen* (1959), that 'it was the Spanish Civil War that obsessed me in the first months of the infant firm and dominated its policy for the next three years', and he published several books on the subject (the best known being George Orwell's *Homage to Catalonia*). A salient feature of the Spanish situation was of course the existence of a mass movement of revolutionary syndicalists led by militant anarchists, and Warburg decided to publish a book on the ideology which inspired them.

In April 1937 – at a time of growing confrontation between the Nationalist rebels and their Falangist allies on one side and the Republican regime and its left-wing allies on the other, and also between the libertarian movement and the Socialist and Communist authorities within the Republic – Warburg approached *Spain and the World*, the new leading anarchist paper in Britain, with a proposal for a short book on anarchism. The suggestion was passed on to Emma Goldman (1869–1940), the best-known anarchist in Europe, who was then working for the Spanish anarcho-syndicalists in London; but, knowing that she had neither the time nor the capacity to produce such a work, she decided to approach someone else instead.

As it happened, there was actually already in existence such a book, or at least the basis for one. This was a long introduction to the subject by Emma Goldman's lifelong friend and colleague Alexander Berkman (1870–1936), which had been written a decade earlier and published in the United States in 1929 in two simultaneous editions as *What is Communist Anarchism?* and as *Now and After: The ABC of Communist Anarchism.* Emma Goldman herself wrote the introduction for a new posthumous edition which was published in the United States in August 1937, so she was well aware of its existence. Moreover, it hadn't yet appeared in Britain, and could easily have been published in a revised form as a new book – indeed a shortened version did appear as a pamphlet a few years later (*ABC of Anarchism*, Freedom Press, 1942, frequently reprinted). But it was much too long for Warburg's purpose, it concentrated on anarchist communism rather than anarcho-syndicalism, and it contained much material on the Russian rather than the Spanish Revolution. Rather than trying to adapt or abridge Berkman's old book, Emma Goldman approached Rudolf Rocker in the United States for a new one.

She wrote telling him about Warburg's proposal and asking him to accept it, and commented:

... A work on Syndicalism in the English language is desperately needed now. It would do tremendous good. The very fact that a publisher asks for such a book shows that he too realises the importance of it ... Rudolf dear you really should do the book.

And you should do it as quickly as possible. After all a short work on Anarcho-Syndicalism is not a work of science or deep philosophy. To reach large masses it must be kept in a light tone. Anyhow you and no one else are the man to do it. And I hope you will undertake it. It will be a real disgrace to refuse such an opportunity to present our ideas before a large public in England and America. Do you not think so? ... Of course you must write it in English. If need be it can be revised here ... I feel certain if you made up your mind you could do it in a month ... Please, please dear Rudolf say Yes ... (4 May 1937)

Rocker liked the idea but he was very busy. He had only recently managed to get his magnum opus, *Nationalism and Culture*, translated into Spanish and then into English (the latter work being started by Alexander Berkman and completed by Ray E. Chase, a retired academic in Los Angeles), and he was at this time involved in the details of its publication in the United States. He, too, was much concerned with Spain; at the beginning of the Civil War he had written a pamphlet on *The Truth about Spain* (1936), and now he was writing another one on *The Tragedy of Spain* (1937). He was also trying to earn his living. He therefore replied after a few days that he would be able to start work on the new book in a few months (23 May 1937).

Meanwhile, since he still wrote in German, he had written to ask Chase whether he would be able to translate it into English. Chase replied favourably: 'Of course I'll be glad to do it for you, if you are sure that I am really the man for the task' (23 May 1937); and he returned to the subject in further letters: 'What of the essay on Anarcho-Syndicalism? Are you going on with it? Am I to translate it?' (15 June 1937); 'I should be very glad to have the job' (30 July 1937).

Emma Goldman replied to Rocker in characteristic style:

I wish I had you here. Believe me I would spank you ... Don't you realise old dear that we never had such a golden opportunity as the offer of the London publisher to get our ideas before a large section of the British workers? And that there never was a more propitious moment than now to make Anarcho-Syndicalism known in this country? ... It's you my dear and you cannot get away from it. Please please set to work on it as quickly as possible. After all you even need no material on the subject. You have got it at your finger tips. You should therefore be able to do it quickly. Won't you try? ... (10 June 1937)

Milly Rocker replied a few days later:

... Believe me that he realise what it means to publish a book on Syndicalism by a publisher, where we could reach quite a different circle of readers, and important it is, it is just wonderful. He will do it with great pleasure, and will do it well, as soon as he is through with the work in hands, and just have one or two swims. Is that good enough darling? Say yes, and smile, do, please. (24 June 1937)

Emma Goldman passed the news of Rocker's acceptance on to Warburg, and sent his contract on to Rocker, who signed and returned it at once – though he changed the delivery date from August to September. She wrote several more letters during the next few months, suggesting what he should write and urging that he should write quickly (23 July and 11 September 1937), and then discussing the progress of the production and publication of the book (19 November and 30 December 1937, 4 January and 22 February 1938).

He wrote the 45,000-word text in German between July and October 1937, sending successive instalments to Chase, who rapidly translated them and sent them on to London, reporting progress back to Rocker: 'I am working on your *Anarchism* ...' (13 September 1937); 'It's going to be hard to make the deadline you said had been set – but I have kept up with you ...' (14 October 1937). The job was finished in December 1937, the book was set up in proof by January 1938, and published in London in March 1938. On the cover and title-page it was called simply *Anarcho-Syndicalism*; but on the red jacket it was described in more detail as *'Anarcho-Syndicalism: Theory & Practice –* An introduction to a subject which the Spanish War has brought into overwhelming prominence'.

There were some private misgivings about the result. Emma Goldman wrote telling Rocker that she had complained about 'the numerous mistakes' to Warburg, who had blamed the proof-readers (29 March 1938). And Chase wrote telling Rocker that he had received his copy of the book, and commented sadly: 'I have had time merely to glance into it. I note that there is no mention of a translator. That, of course, is unimportant, but it seems a trifle odd ...' (5 May 1938).

But the public reception was good, and the reviews were generally favourable. The most authoritative independent one appeared in the *Times Literary Supplement* on 23 April 1938 (unsigned, but written by E. H. Carr):

Anarcho-Syndicalism, as presented in this earnest but somewhat heavily written little book, is on the one hand a restatement of essential Liberal doctrine in modern terms and on the other a reaction against the form which the Socialist movement has assumed. It is anarchist in so far as it aims at freeing mankind from the coercion of the State, which is to be replaced by a federation of communities, and it is syndicalist in so far as it proposes to free the workers in industry from employers' control and to place economic power in the hands of the trade unions. Mr Rocker, who is the philosopher of the movement, traces back its beginnings to Godwin and Proudhon and finds its modern inspiration in Bakunin and Kropotkin. It is interesting to note how many modern thinkers find in Kropotkin's study of what may be called collective security in the animal world the answer to the cruder political inferences drawn from the doctrine of the survival of the fittest.

Having set out his principles, Mr Rocker fortifies them by an account of England under industrialism in which all the shadows are energetically inked in. The narrative overstates the influence of Socialistic ideas in the England of the 'thirties and 'forties, just as it overstates the influence of the First International on the Continent a few years later. The present phase of the movement, we learn, is represented by the various national branches of the International Workingmen's Association. The most important of them is the Spanish Confederacion Nacional del Trabajo (CNT), to whose work in freeing Catalonia from Fascist reaction Mr Rocker pays a whole-hearted tribute on which recent events have passed their commentary.

All this part of the argument is directed against political socialism which in Russia has led to the re-establishment of the coercive State in a strengthened form. The workman's power, Mr

Rocker insists, is economic and its weapon is the strike. In this connexion we are told that 'the great general strike of the English workers in 1926 was the result of a planned attempt by the employers to lower the general standard of living by cutting wages.' The value of the book is much diminished by the exaggerations, of which this sentence is a flagrant example.

The book was warmly welcomed by the anarchist movement. A Spanish translation by the leading libertarian intellectual Diego Abad de Santillan was published in Barcelona during 1938. In Britain the leading libertarian intellectual Herbert Read wrote a long joint review of *Anarcho-Syndicalism* and *Nationalism and Culture* in *The Criterion* (July 1938). But the most authoritative review appeared, as might be expected, in *Spain and the World*, on 18 March 1938, being printed in bold type and written by the editor, 'V. R.' (Vernon Richards). He began by describing the interest in anarchism created by events in Spain and mentioning some of the books already published on various aspects of the subject, and continued:

> But what was really needed was a complete work on Anarcho-Syndicalism, in which the subject would be dealt with in all its aspects. In *Anarcho-Syndicalism* by Rudolf Rocker we at last have the book. It has no pretension of being complete in detail; that would need a much longer book. However it is as well that the book is short, for by its brevity it succeeds more successfully in its aim: to briefly explain Anarcho-Syndicalism to the uninitiated – and the initiated.

After a summary of the book, he concluded:

> The above is but a brief account of Rudolf Rocker's excellent book. It is impossible, in the space available to bring out all the detail which it contains. *Anarcho-Syndicalism* should be read by all who wish to become acquainted with the subject, for an understanding of Anarcho-Syndicalism. So far the few books which have been written during the past two years have been generous in their distortion of the objectives and the work carried on by the Anarchists for the achievement of true Socialism; this is understandable, for the authors have been

communists! *Anarcho-Syndicalism* on the other hand is written by
one whose life has been dedicated to the Anarchist ideal and
struggle, both in Germany and in America.

In fact the book wasn't a commercial success at all (nor was
Homage to Catalonia). Within a couple of years the Freedom Press
acquired the remaindered stock (as of several other Warburg books),
and sold it at a reduced price. It wasn't reprinted in Britain or
published in the United States at that time, but after the war a new
edition appeared in India.

Arya Bhavan, an elderly Bombay journalist who had first
contacted Rocker and read the book in 1938, moved from socialism
towards anarchism, founded a libertarian publishing house, and
produced a series of reprints of anarchist classics. During 1947 he
wrote several letters to Rocker. He told him that he wanted to
publish *Anarcho-Syndicalism,* and added: 'Can you not send an
epilogue to it as that will increase the value of the book in this
changed circumstances' (14 April 1947). He wrote again a few weeks
later: 'I am printing here your *Anarcho-Syndicalism.* It will be out in
a couple of months. Can you not oblige me with an epilogue from
you' (9 May 1947). When Rocker agreed, he replied that he was
'indebted to you for writing an epilogue for *Anarcho-Syndicalism.*
The book is almost complete ... Much water has flowed under the
bridge since you wrote *Anarcho-Syndicalism* and your epilogue will
bring it to date' (1 June 1947). And when he received the epilogue,
dated June 1947, he wrote again: 'I am trying to see if it can be
added at the end' (24 July 1947). The book was published by
Modern Publishers in Indore in August, and did include Rocker's
epilogue, as well as a publisher's introduction (and many more
misprints).

Incidentally, Rocker never made any money from the book. His
small advance royalty from Warburg (£25) just covered the
translation fee for Chase ($100); he received nothing from India.

In 1946 Rocker wrote an abridged version of the book as an essay
with the title *Anarchism and Anarcho-Syndicalism* for Feliks Gross's
American symposium *European Ideologies* (1948), consisting of
slightly revised passages from different parts of the book and
amounting to nearly one-third of the text. This was reprinted in
James J. Martin's edition of Paul Eltzbacher's *Anarchism* (1960),
extracts were included in two American anthologies – Irving Louis

Horowitz's *The Anarchists* (1964) and Priscilla Long's *The New Left* (1969) – and it was later published as a pamphlet. Extracts from the original book were also included in another American anthology – Leonard I. Krimerman's and Lewis Perry's *Patterns of Anarchy* (1966) – and various extracts and versions have appeared in different forms from time to time.

During recent years there have been an expensive American reprint of the Indian edition (Gordon Press, 1972) and a cheap (slightly abridged) British reprint of the British one (Phoenix Press, 1987). The present edition gives a full photographic reprint of the text of the original British edition of 1938, together with a corrected verbatim transcript of the epilogue to the Indian edition of 1947, with the addition of Noam Chomsky's new preface and this new introduction. Rocker's account of anarchism and especially of its syndicalist variety is inevitably dated in its general emphasis and in some particular points, and it does include several minor errors (especially in proper names and quotations), but after half a century it remains valuable as a short and clear view of a significant ideology by one of its best-known and best-informed adherents.

A convenient summary of the later history of the international anarcho-syndicalist movement is given by C. Longmore's pamphlet *The IWA Today: A Short Account of the International Workers Association and Its Sections* (South London Direct Action Movement, 1985). This describes the formation and early development of the International Working Men's Association, and the crisis of the Second World War, as discussed in more detail by Rocker, and then takes up the story from the first post-war congress in Toulouse in 1951. The International Workers Association – the original English title was amended for anti-sexist reasons – declined to its lowest point during the 1960s, under the double pressure this time of Communism and capitalism. It revived during the early 1980s, following the revival of libertarian rebellion around the world during the late 1960s and especially the revival of the Spanish movement during the late 1970s; at the congress of Madrid in 1984 it comprised a dozen national or regional sections.

In Britain, which was rather neglected by Rocker, there was a vigorous syndicalist movement before the First World War with strong libertarian tendencies – especially among the Jewish workers in East London, where Rocker himself was so influential – and there were several attempts to form a specifically anarcho-syndicalist organisation during the 1930s. The Anarchist Federation of Britain turned towards syndicalism after the Second World War and became the Syndicalist Workers Federation in 1950, but this too declined. However it was later revived as the Anarchist Syndicalist Alliance and then in 1979 as the Direct Action Movement, which has been involved in several industrial struggles.

However, the basic principles of anarcho-syndicalism – self-management, autonomy, direct action, spontaneity, mutual aid, libertarianism in general – are nowadays represented not so much by the militant working-class movement as by other social and political movements which transcend class loyalties. Obvious examples include peace and green movements, youth and student movements, women's and gay movements, communalist and cooperative movements, and the informal manifestations of the spirit of revolt which have revived the old attitudes of nihilism and bohemianism in the alternative and underground culture. If the traditionalist concept of anarchism expounded by Rocker has been continued in the International Workers Association and by such writers as Daniel Guérin and Noam Chomsky, more revisionist concepts which were pioneered by many libertarians during the nineteenth century, and which have been expounded and developed by several writers down to Murray Bookchin and Colin Ward in our own day, should also be taken into consideration in any attempt at a balanced account of anarchism. Nevertheless Rocker, in seeing anarchism primarily as a product of libertarian tendencies in the labour movement and anarcho-syndicalism as the final result of this process, was giving a true picture of the emergence first of the historical anarchist movement during the late nineteenth century and then of one of its most important forms during the early twentieth century (though he himself had increasing doubts about the value of syndicalism, especially towards the end of his life). So his exposition of anarcho-syndicalism at the peak of its influence is both a precious document of its time and a valuable reminder in our time of the continuing importance of an essential element in the complex ideology of anarchism.

Nicolas Walter
London, 1988

Further Reading

Rudolf Rocker's writings were published mainly in German and Yiddish, and also in Spanish, and few were ever translated into English; similarly, there is no proper account of his life or study of his work in English. The English translation of the relevant section of his memoirs, *The London Years* (1956), has long been out of print. British editions of several works – Rocker's *Nationalism and Culture* (1937, 1947, 1978), Paul Eltzbacher's *Anarchism* (1960) and Rocker's *Anarchism and Anarcho-Syndicalism* (1973, 1988) – have been produced or distributed by the Freedom Press.

Anarcho-syndicalist organisations have produced many introductory pamphlets which are obtainable from them or from sympathetic bookshops. There is no scholarly account in English of anarcho-syndicalism as such, but there is useful material in some books on anarchism in general and there are some studies of the syndicalist movements in various countries. Rocker's own bibliography (pages 155–8), which contains a fair selection of works published before 1938, may be supplemented as follows.

Bertrand Russell's *Roads to Freedom* (first published in 1918), which is included in Rocker's list, appeared in many later editions and is still an excellent short analysis of socialism, anarchism and syndicalism. J. A. Estey's *Revolutionary Syndicalism* (1913), which was omitted from Rocker's list, is a detailed account of the theory at that time. Among the many English-language histories and anthologies of anarchism, the most widely read are George Woodcock's *Anarchism* (first published in 1962) and *The Anarchist Reader* (first published in 1977), paperback editions being available respectively from Penguin Books and Fontana Books. A more penetrating study is Daniel Guérin's *Anarchism: From Theory to Practice* (1970), Mary Klopper's translation of a book first published in France in 1965, with an introduction by Noam Chomsky; unfortunately Guérin's enormous anthology, *Ni dieu, ni maître*, also first published in France in 1965, has never been translated into English. There is some relevant material in my pamphlet *About Anarchism* (first published in 1969), and in *Anarchism Today* (1971), a symposium edited by David E. Apter and James Joll.

The French movement is described in F. F. Ridley, *Revolutionary Syndicalism in France* (1970). There is no single study of Spanish anarcho-syndicalism, but particularly useful books are Gerald

Brenan, *The Spanish Labyrinth* (1943); Murray Bookchin, *The Spanish Anarchists: The Heroic Years, 1868–1936* (1977); Juan Gomez Casas, *Anarchist Organisation: The History of the FAI* (1986); Pierre Broué and Emile Témime, *The Revolution and the Civil War in Spain* (1972); José Peirats, *Anarchists in the Spanish Revolution* (1977). Material on anarcho-syndicalism in various parts of Latin America appears in Victor Alba, *Politics and the Labour Movement in Latin America* (1968), and in books on particular countries: Ronaldo Munck, *Argentina: From Anarchism to Peronism* (1987); John W. F. Dulles, *Anarchists and Communists in Brazil, 1900–1935* (1973); John M. Hart, *Anarchism and the Mexican Working Class, 1860–1931* (1978). The Russian movement is described in Paul Avrich, *The Russian Anarchists* (1967).

The American movement is described in Patrick Renshaw, *The Wobblies* (1967), and Melvyn Dubofsky, *We Shall Be All* (1969), and in Joyce Kornbluh's anthology, *Rebel Voices* (1964). The British movement is described in Bob Holton, *British Syndicalism, 1900–1914* (1976) and John Quail, *The Slow Burning Fuse* (1977). The Jewish movement in Britain is described in W. J. Fishman's *East End Jewish Radicals* (1975).

Acknowledgements

Thanks are due to: Fermin Rocker, the younger son and literary executor of Rudolf Rocker, for giving permission to make use of his father's writings and for helpful comments; the International Institute of Social History, Amsterdam, for the use of its resources and for permission to make use of unpublished material in its possession (the Rudolf Rocker Collection contains manuscripts of several of his books and letters to him, and the Emma Goldman Collection contains letters to and from her); and Paul Avrich, Heiner Becker, David Goodway, Vernon Richards and Christine Walter for help of various kinds. An earlier version of this introduction appeared in *The Raven* 4 (February 1988).

1

ANARCHISM: ITS AIMS AND PURPOSES

Anarchism versus economic monopoly and state power ; Forerunners of modern Anarchism ; William Godwin and his work on Political Justice ; P. J. Proudhon and his idea of political and economic decentralisation ; Max Stirner's work, The Ego and Its Own ; M. Bakunin the Collectivist and founder of the anarchist movement ; P. Kropotkin the exponent of Anarchist Communism and the philosophy of Mutual Aid ; Anarchism and Revolution ; Anarchism a synthesis of Socialism and Liberalism ; Anarchism versus Economic Materialism and Dictatorship ; Anarchism and the State ; Anarchism a tendency in history ; Freedom and Culture.

ANARCHISM is a definite intellectual current in the life of our time, whose adherents advocate the abolition of economic monopolies and of all political and social coercive institutions within society. In place of the present capitalistic economic order Anarchists would have a free association of all productive forces based upon co-operative labour, which would have as its sole purpose the satisfying of the necessary requirements of every member of society, and would no longer have in view the special interest of privileged minorities within the social union. In place of the present state-organizations with their lifeless machinery of political and bureaucratic institutions Anarchists desire a federation of free com-

munities which shall be bound to one another by their
common economic and social interests and shall arrange
their affairs by mutual agreement and free contract.

Anyone who studies at all profoundly the economic and
political development of the present social system will
easily recognize that these objectives do not spring from
the Utopian ideas of a few imaginative innovators, but
that they are the logical outcome of a thorough examination of the present day social maladjustments, which with
every new phase of the existing social conditions manifest
themselves more plainly and more unwholesomely.
Modern monopoly, capitalism and the totalitarian state
are merely the last terms in a development which could
culminate in no other results.

The portentous development of our present economic
system, leading to a mighty accumulation of social wealth
in the hands of privileged minorities and to a continuous
impoverishment of the great masses of the people,
prepared the way for the present political and social
reaction, and befriended it in every way. It sacrificed
the general interests of human society to the private
interests of individuals, and thus systematically under-
mined the relationship between man and man. People
forgot that industry is not an end in itself, but should be
only a means to insure to man his material subsistence and
to make accessible to him the blessings of a higher
intellectual culture. Where industry is everything and
man is nothing begins the realm of a ruthless economic
despotism whose workings are no less disastrous than
those of any political despotism. The two mutually
augment one another, and they are fed from the same
source.

The economic dictatorship of the monopolies and the
political dictatorship of the totalitarian state are the out-

growth of the same social objectives, and the directors of both have the presumption to try to reduce all the countless expressions of social life to the mechanical tempo of the machine and to tune everything organic to the lifeless rhythm of the political apparatus. Our modern social system has split the social organism in every country into hostile classes internally, and externally it has broken the common cultural circle up into hostile nations ; and both classes and nations confront one another with open antagonism and by their ceaseless warfare keep the communal social life in continual convulsions. The late World War and its terrible after effects, which are themselves only the results of the present struggles for economic and political power, and the constant dread of new wars, which to-day dominates all peoples, are only the logical consequences of this unendurable condition, which will inevitably lead us to a universal catastrophe, if social development does not take a new course soon enough. The mere fact that most states are obliged to-day to spend from fifty to seventy per cent. of their annual income for so-called national defence and the liquidation of old war debts is proof of the untenability of the present status, and should make clear to everybody that the alleged protection which the state affords the individual is certainly purchased too dearly.

The ever growing power of a soulless political bureaucracy which supervises and safeguards the life of man from the cradle to the grave is putting ever greater obstacles in the way of the solidaric co-operation of human beings and crushing out every possibility of new development. A system which in every act of its life sacrifices the welfare of large sections of the people, yes, of whole nations, to the selfish lust for power and the

economic interests of small minorities must of necessity
dissolve all social ties and lead to a constant war of each
against all. This system has been merely the pace-
maker for the great intellectual and social reaction which
finds its expression to-day in modern Fascism, far sur-
passing the obsession for power of the absolute monarchy
of past centuries and seeking to bring every sphere of
human activity under the control of the state. Just as
for the various systems of religious theology God is
everything and man nothing, so for this modern political
theology, the state is everything and the subject nothing.
And just as behind the " will of God " there always lay
hidden the will of privileged minorities, so to-day there
hides behind the " will of the state " only the selfish
interest of those who feel called to interpret this will in
their own sense and to force it upon the people

Anarchist ideas are to be found in every period of
known history, although there still remains a good deal
of work for historical research in this field. We encounter
them in the Chinese sage, Lao-tse (The Course and The
Right Way) and in the later Greek philosophers, the
Hedonists and Cynics and other advocates of so-called
" natural right," and in particular in Zeno who, at the
opposite pole from Plato, founded the Stoic school.
They found expression in the teaching of the Gnostic,
Karpocrates, in Alexandria, and had an unmistakable
influence on certain Christian sects of the Middle Ages
in France, Germany, and Holland, almost all of which
fell victims to the most savage persecutions. In the
history of the Bohemian reformation they found a powerful champion in Peter Chelčicky, who in his work, " The
Net of Faith," passed the same judgment on the church

and the state as Tolstoi did later. Among the great
Humanists there was Rabelais, who in his description of
the happy Abbey of Thélème (Gargantua) presented a
picture of life freed from all authoritative restraints.
Of other pioneers of libertarian thinking we will mention
here only La Boétie, Sylvain Maréchal, and, above all,
Diderot, in whose volumionus writings one finds thickly
strewn the utterances of a truly great mind which had
rid itself of every authoritarian prejudice.

Meanwhile, it was reserved for more recent history
to give clear form to the Anarchist conception of life
and to connect it with the immediate processes of social
evolution. This was done for the first time in William
Godwin's splendidly conceived work, *Concerning Political
Justice and its Influence upon General Virtue and Happiness*,
London, 1793. Godwin's work was, we might say, the
ripened fruit of that long evolution of the concepts of
political and social radicalism in England which proceeds
in a continuous line from George Buchanan through
Richard Hooker, Gerard Winstanley, Algernon Sidney,
John Locke, Robert Wallace, and John Bellers to Jeremy
Bentham, Joseph Priestley, Richard Price, and Thomas
Paine.

Godwin recognized very clearly that the cause of social
evils is to be sought, not in the form of the state, but in
its very existence. Just as the state presents only a
caricature of a genuine society, so also it makes of human
beings who are held under its eternal guardianship
merely caricatures of their real selves by constantly com-
pelling them to repress their natural inclinations and
holding them to things that are repugnant to their inner
impulses. Only in this way is it possible to mould
human beings to the established form of good subjects.
A normal human being who was not interfered with in

his natural development would of himself shape the environment that suits his inborn demand for peace and freedom.

But Godwin also recognized that human beings can only live together naturally and freely when the proper economic conditions for this are given, and when the individual is no longer subject to exploitation by another, a consideration which the representatives of mere political radicalism almost wholly overlooked. Hence they were later compelled to make constantly greater concessions to that power of the state which they had wished to restrict to a minimum. Godwin's idea of a stateless society assumed the social ownership of all natural and social wealth, and the carrying on of economic life by the free co-operation of the producers ; in this sense he was really the founder of the later communist Anarchism.

Godwin's work had a very strong influence on advanced circles of the English workers and the more enlightened sections of the liberal intelligentsia. Most important of all, he contributed to give to the young Socialist movement in England, which found its maturest exponents in Robert Owen, John Gray, and William Thompson, that unmistakably libertarian character which it had for a long time, and which it never assumed in Germany and many other countries.

But a far greater influence on the development of Anarchist theory was that of Pierre Joseph Proudhon, one of the most intellectually gifted and certainly the most many-sided writer of whom modern Socialism can boast. Proudhon was completely rooted in the intellectual and social life of his period, and these inspired his attitude upon every question he dealt with. Therefore, he is not to be judged, as he has been even by many of his later followers, by his special practical proposals,

which were born of the needs of the hour. Among the
numerous Socialist thinkers of his time he was the one
who understood most profoundly the cause of social
maladjustment, and possessed, besides, the greatest
breadth of vision. He was the outspoken opponent of
all systems, and saw in social evolution the eternal urge to
new and higher forms of intellectual and social life, and
it was his conviction that this evolution could not be
bound by any definite abstract formulas.

Proudhon opposed the influence of the Jacobin tradition, which dominated the thinking of the French
democrats and of most of the Socialists of that period
with the same determination as the interference of the
central state and economic monopoly in the natural
processes of social advance. To rid society of those two
cancerous growths was for him the great task of the
nineteenth-century revolution. Proudhon was no communist. He condemned property as merely the privilege
of exploitation, but he recognized the ownership of the
instruments of labour by all, made effective through
industrial groups bound to one another by free contract,
so long as this right was not made to serve the exploitation
of others and as long as the full product of his individual
labour was assured to every human being. This organization based on reciprocity (mutualité) guarantees the enjoy-
ment of equal rights by each in exchange for equal
services. The average working time required for the
completion of any product becomes the measure of its
value and is the basis of mutual exchange. In this way
capital is deprived of its usurial power and is completely
bound up with the performance of work. By being
made available to all it ceases to be an instrument for
exploitation.

Such a form of economy makes any political coercive

apparatus superfluous. Society becomes a league of
free communities which arrange their affairs according
to need, by themselves or in association with others, and
in which man's freedom finds in the equal freedom of
others not its limitation, but its security and confirma-
tion. " The freer, the more independent and enter-
prising the individual is in a society, the better for the
society." This organization of Federalism in which
Proudhon saw the immediate future of mankind sets no
definite limitations on further possibilities of development,
and offers the widest scope to every individual and social
activity. Starting out from the point of view of the
Federation, Proudhon combated likewise the asperations
for political unity of the awakening nationalism of the
time, and in particular of that nationalism which found in
Mazzini, Garibaldi, Lelewel, and others such strong
advocates. In this respect also he saw more clearly
than most of his contemporaries. Proudhon exerted a
strong influence on the development of Socialism, which
made itself felt especially in the Latin countries. But
the so-called individual Anarchism, which found able
exponents in America in such men as Josiah Warren,
Stephen Pearl Andrews, William B. Greene, Lysander
Spooner, Francis D. Tandy, and most notably in Ben-
jamin R. Tucker ran in similar lines, though none of its
representatives could approach Proudhon's breadth of
view.

Anarchism found a unique expression in Max Stirner's
(Johann Kaspar Schmidt's) book, *Der Einzige und sein
Eigentum* (The Ego and His Own), which, it is true,
quickly passed into oblivion and had no influence at all
on the Anarchist movement as such—though it was to
experience an unexpected resurrection fifty years later.
Stirner's book is pre-eminently a philosophic work,

which traces man's dependence on so-called higher powers through all its devious ways, and is not timid about drawing inferences from the knowledge gained by the survey. It is the book of a conscious and deliberate insurgent, which reveals no reverence for any authority, however exalted, and therefore impels powerfully to independent thinking.

Anarchism found a virile champion of vigorous revolutionary energy in Michael Bakunin, who took his stand upon the teachings of Proudhon, but extended them on the economic side when he, along with the collectivist wing of the First International, came out for the collective ownership of the land and of all other means of production, and wished to restrict the right of private ownership to the full product of individual labour. Bakunin also was an opponent of Communism, which in his time had a thoroughly authoritarian character, like that which it has again assumed to-day in Bolshevism. In one of his four speeches at the Congress of the *League for Peace and Freedom* in Bern (1868), he said : " I am not a Communist because Communism unites all the forces of society in the state and becomes absorbed in it ; because it inevitably leads to the concentration of all property in the hands of the state, while I seek the abolition of the state—the complete elimination of the principle of authority and governmental guardianship, which under the pretence of making men moral and civilizing them, has up to now always enslaved, oppressed, exploited, and ruined them."

Bakunin was a determined revolutionary and did not believe in an amicable adjustment of the existing class conflict. He recognized that the ruling classes blindly and stubbornly opposed even the slightest social reform, and accordingly saw the only salvation in an international social revolution, which should abolish all the ecclesiastical, political, military, bureaucratic, and judicial institutions of the existing social system and introduce in their stead a federation of free workers' associations to provide for the requirements of daily life.   Since he, like so many of his contemporaries, believed in the close proximity of the Revolution, he directed all his vast energy to combining all the genuinely revolutionary and libertarian elements within and without the *International* to safeguard the coming revolution against any dictatorship or any retrogression to the old conditions.   Thus he became in a very special sense the creator of the modern Anarchist movement.

Anarchism found a valuable advocate in Peter Kropotkin, who set himself the task of making the achievements of modern natural science available for the development of the sociological concepts of Anarchism.   In his ingenious book, *Mutual Aid—a Factor of Evolution*, he entered the lists against so-called *Social Darwinism*, whose exponents tried to prove the inevitability of the existing social conditions from the Darwinian theory of the struggle for existence by raising the struggle of the strong against the weak to the status of an iron law for all natural processes, to which even man is subject.   In reality this conception was strongly influenced by the Malthusian doctrine that life's table is not spread for all, and that the unneeded will just have to reconcile themselves to this fact.

Kropotkin showed that this conception of nature as a field of unrestricted warfare is only a caricature of real life, and that along with the brutal struggle for existence, which is fought out with tooth and claw, there exists in nature also another principle which is expressed in the social combination of the weaker species and the maintenance of races by the evolution of social instincts and mutual aid.

In this sense man is not the creator of society, but society the creator of man, for he inherited from the species that preceded him the social instinct which alone enabled him to maintain himself in his first environment against the physical superiority of other species, and to make sure of an undreamed-of height of development. This second tendency in the struggle for existence is far superior to the first, as is shown by the steady retrogression of those species which have no social life and are dependent merely upon their physical strength. This view, which to-day is meeting with constantly wider acceptance in the natural sciences and in social research, opened wholly new vistas to speculation concerning human evolution.

The fact is that even under the worst despotism most of man's personal relations with his fellows are arranged by free agreement and solidaric co-operation, without which social life would not be possible at all. If this were not the case even the strongest coercive arrangements of the state would not be able to maintain the social order for a single day. However, these natural forms of behaviour, which arise from man's inmost nature, are to-day constantly interfered with and crippled by the effects of economic exploitation and governmental guardianship, which represents in human society the brutal form of the struggle for existence, which has to be overcome by the other form of mutual aid and free co-operation. The consciousness of personal responsibility and that other precious good that has come down to man by inheritance from remote antiquity : that capacity for sympathy with others in which all social ethics, all ideas of social justice, have their origin, develop best in freedom.

Like Bakunin, Kropotkin too was a revolutionary.
But he, like Élisée Reclus and others, saw in revolution
only a special phase of the evolutionary process, which
appears when new social aspirations are so restricted in
their natural development by authority that they have to
shatter the old shell by violence before they can function
as new factors in human life.   In contrast to Proudhon
and Bakunin, Kropotkin advocated community ownership, not only of the means of production, but of the
products of labour as well, as it was his opinion that in
the present status of technique no exact measure of the
value of individual labour is possible, but that, on the
other hand, by a rational direction of our modern
methods of labour it will be possible to assure comparative
abundance to every human being.   Communist Anarchism, which before him had already been urged by Joseph
Dejacque, Élisée Reclus, Errico Malatesta, Carlo Cafiero,
and others, and which is advocated by the great majority
of Anarchists to-day, found in him one of its most brilliant
exponents.

Mention must also be made here of Leo Tolstoi, who
took from primitive Christianity and, on the basis of the
ethical principles laid down in the gospels, arrived at
the idea of a society without rulership.[1]

Common to all Anarchists is the desire to free society
of all political and social coercive institutions which
stand in the way of the development of a free humanity.
In this sense Mutualism, Collectivism, and Communism
are not to be regarded as closed systems permitting no
further development, but merely as economic assumptions
as to the means of safeguarding a free community.   There

---

[1] The reader will find in the works of Max Nettlau listed in the
bibliography a very well informed history of Anarchist doctrines
and movements.

will even probably be in the society of the future different forms of economic co-operation existing side by side, since any social progress must be associated with that free experimentation and practical testing-out for which in a society of free communities there will be afforded every opportunity.

The same holds true for the various methods of Anarchism. Most Anarchists of our time are convinced that a social transformation of society cannot be brought about without violent revolutionary convulsions. The violence of these convulsions, of course, depends upon the strength of the resistance which the ruling classes will be able to oppose to the realization of the new ideas. The wider the circles which are inspired with the idea of a reorganization of society in the spirit of freedom and Socialism, the easier will be the birth pains of the coming social revolution.

In modern Anarchism we have the confluence of the two great currents which during and since the French Revolution have found such characteristic expression in the intellectual life of Europe : Socialism and Liberalism. Modern Socialism developed when profound observers of social life came to see more and more clearly that political constitutions and changes in the form of government could never get to the bottom of that great problem that we call " the social question." Its supporters recognized that a social equalizing of human beings, despite the loveliest of theoretical assumptions, is not possible so long as people are separated into classes on the basis of their owning or not owning property, classes whose mere existence excludes in advance any thought of a genuine community. And so there developed the

recognition that only by elimination of economic monopolies and common ownership of the means of production,
in a word, by a complete transformation of all economic
conditions and social institutions associated with them,
does a condition of social justice become thinkable, a
status in which society shall become a genuine community,
and human labour shall no longer serve the ends of
exploitation, but shall serve to assure abundance to everyone. But as soon as Socialism began to assemble its
forces and became a movement, there at once came to
light certain differences of opinion due to the influence
of the social environment in different countries. It is a
fact that every political concept from theocracy to Cæsar-
ism and dictatorship have affected certain factions in the
Socialist movement. Meanwhile, there have been two
great currents in political thought which have been of
decisive significance for the development of Socialistic
ideas : Liberalism, which powerfully stimulated advanced
minds in the Anglo-Saxon countries and Spain, in particular, and Democracy in the later sense to which Rousseau
gave expression in his *Social Contract,* and which found
its most influential representatives in the leaders of
French Jacobinism. While Liberalism in its social
theorizing started off from the individual and wished to
limit the state's activities to a minimum, Democracy
took its stand on an abstract collective concept, Rousseau's
" general will," which it sought to fix in the national
state.

Liberalism and Democracy were pre-eminently political
concepts, and, since the great majority of the original
adherents of both maintained the right of ownership in
the old sense, these had to renounce them both when
economic development took a course which could not be
practically reconciled with the original principles of

Democracy, and still less with those of Liberalism.
Democracy with its motto of " equality of all citizens
before the law," and Liberalism with its " right of man
over his own person," both shipwrecked on the realities
of the capitalist economic form. So long as millions of
human beings in every country had to sell their labour-
power to a small minority of owners, and to sink into the
most wretched misery if they could find no buyers, the
so-called " equality before the law " remains merely a
pious fraud, since the laws are made by those who find
themselves in possession of the social wealth. But in
the same way there can also be no talk of a " right over
one's own person," for that right ends when one is compelled to submit to the economic dictation of another
if he does not want to starve.

Anarchism has in common with Liberalism the idea
that the happiness and prosperity of the individual must
be the standard in all social matters. And, in common
with the great representatives of Liberal thought, it has
also the idea of limiting the functions of government
to a minimum. Its supporters have followed this thought
to its ultimate logical consequences, and wish to eliminate
every institution of political power from the life of
society. When Jefferson clothes the basic concept of
Liberalism in the words : " That government is best
which governs least," then Anarchists say with Thoreau :
" That government is best which governs not at all."

In common with the founders of Socialism, Anarchists
demand the abolition of all economic monopolies and the
common ownership of the soil and all other means of
production, the use of which must be available to all
without distinction ; for personal and social freedom is
conceivable only on the basis of equal economic advantages
for everybody. Within the Socialist movement itself

the Anarchist represent the viewpoint that the war against
capitalism must be at the same time a war against all
institutions of political power, for in history economic
exploitation has always gone hand in hand with political
and social oppression. The exploitation of man by man
and the dominion of man over man are inseparable, and
each is the condition of the other.

As long as within society a possessing and a non-
possessing group of human beings face one another in
enmity, the state will be indispensable to the possessing
minority for the protection of its privileges. When this
condition of social injustice vanishes to give place to a
higher order of things, which shall recognize no special
rights and shall have as its basic assumption the community of social interests, government over men must
yield the field to the administration of economic and social
affairs, or, to speak with Saint Simon : " The time will
come when the art of governing men will disappear. A
new art will take its place, the art of administering
things."

And this disposes of the theory maintained by Marx
and his followers that the state, in the form of a proletarian
dictatorship, is a necessary transitional stage to a classless
society, in which the state after the elimination of all
class conflicts and then of classes themselves, will dissolve
itself and vanish from the canvas. This concept, which
completely mistakes the real nature of the state and the
significance in history of the factor of political power,
is only the logical outcome of so-called economic
materialism, which sees in all the phenomena of history
merely the inevitable effects of the methods of production
of the time. Under the influence of this theory people
came to regard the different forms of the state and all
other social institutions as a " juridical and political

superstructure " on the " economic edifice " of society, and thought that they had found in that theory the key to every historic process. In reality every section of history affords us thousands of examples of the way in which the economic development of a country has been set back for centuries and forced into prescribed forms by particular struggles for political power.

Before the rise of the ecclesiastical monarchy Spain was industrially the most advanced country in Europe and held the first place in economic production in almost every field. But a century after the triumph of the Christian monarchy most of its industries had disappeared. What was left of them survived only in the most wretched condition. In most industries they had reverted to the most primitive methods of production. Agriculture collapsed, canals and waterways fell into ruin, and vast stretches of country were transformed into deserts. Down to this day Spain has never recovered from that set-back. The aspirations of a particular caste for political power had laid economic development fallow for centuries.

Princely absolutism in Europe, with its silly " economic ordinances " and " industrial legislation," which punished severely any deviation from the prescribed methods of production and permitted no new inventions, blocked industrial progress in European countries for centuries, and prevented its natural development. And were there not considerations of political power which after the World War constantly balked any escape from the universal economic crisis and delivered the future of whole countries to politics-playing generals and political adventurers ? Who will assert that modern Fascism was an inevitable result of economic development ?

In Russia, however, where the so-called " proletarian dictatorship " has ripened into reality, the aspirations of

a particular party for political power have prevented
any truly socialistic reconstruction of economy and have
forced the country into the slavery of a grinding state-
capitalism. The " dictatorship of the proletariat," in
which naïve souls wish to see merely a passing, but
inevitable, transition stage to real Socialism, has to-day
grown into a frightful despotism, which lags behind the
tyranny of the Fascist states in nothing.

The assertion that the state must continue to exist
until class conflicts, and classes with them, disappear,
sounds, in the light of all historical experience, almost
like a bad joke. Every type of political power pre-
supposes some particular form of human slavery, for
the maintenance of which it is called into being. Just
as outwardly, that is, in relation to other states, the state
has to create certain artificial antagonisms in order to
justify its existence, so also internally the cleavage of
society into castes, ranks, and classes is an essential
condition of its continuance. The state is capable only
of protecting old privileges and creating new ones ; in
that its whole significance is exhausted.

A new state which has been brought into existence by
a social revolution can put an end to the privileges of
the old ruling classes, but it can do this only by
immediately setting up a new privileged class, which it
will require for the maintenance of its rulership. The
development of the Bolshevist bureaucracy in Russia
under the alleged dictatorship of the proletariat—which
has never been anything but the dictatorship of a small
clique *over* the proletariat and the entire Russian people
—is merely a new instance of an old historical experience
which has repeated itself uncountable times. This new
ruling class, which to-day is rapidly growing into a new
aristocracy, is set apart from the great masses of Russian

peasants and workers just as clearly as are the privileged castes and classes in other countries from the mass of their peoples.

It could perhaps be objected that the new Russian commissar-ocracy cannot be put upon the same footing as the powerful financial and industrial oligarchies of capitalist states. But the objection will not hold. It is not the size nor the extent of the privilege that matters, but its immediate effect on the daily life of the average human being. An American working-man who, under moderately decent working conditions, earns enough to feed, clothe, and house himself humanly and has enough left over to provide himself with some cultured enjoyments, feels the possession of millions by the Mellons and Morgans less than a man who earns hardly enough to satisfy his most urgent necessities feels the privileges of a little caste of bureaucrats, even if these are not millionaires. People who can scarcely get enough dry bread to satisfy their hunger, who live in squalid rooms which they are often obliged to share with strangers, and who, on top of this, are compelled to work under an intensified speed-up system which raises their productive capacity to the utmost, can but feel the privileges of an upper class which lacks nothing, much more keenly than their class comrades in capitalist countries. And this situation becomes still more unbearable when a despotic state denies to the lower classes the right to complain of existing conditions, so that any protest is made at the risk of their lives.

But even a far greater degree of economic equality than exists in Russia would still be no guarantee against political and social oppression. Economic equality alone is not social liberation. It is just this which Marxism and all the other schools of authoritarian

Socialism have never understood. Even in prison, in the cloister, or in the barracks one finds a fairly high degree of economic equality, as all the inmates are provided with the same dwelling, the same food, the same uniform, and the same tasks. The ancient Inca state in Peru and the Jesuit state in Paraguay had brought equal economic provision for every inhabitant to a fixed system, but in spite of this the vilest despotism prevailed there, and the human being was merely the automaton of a higher will, on whose decisions he had not the slightest influence. It was not without reason that Proudhon saw in a " Socialism " without freedom the worst form of slavery. The urge for social justice can only develop properly and be effective, when it grows out of man's sense of personal freedom and is based on that. In other words *Socialism will be free, or it will not be at all.* In its recognition of this lies the genuine and profound justification for the existence of Anarchism.

Institutions serve the same purpose in the life of society as bodily organs do in plants or animals : they are the organs of the social body. Organs do not arise arbitrarily, but because of the definite necessities of the physical and social environment. The eye of a deep-sea fish is formed very differently from that of an animal that lives on land, because it has to satisfy quite different demands. Changed conditions of life produce changed organs. But an organ always performs the function it was evolved to perform, or a related one. And it gradually disappears or becomes rudimentary as soon as its function is no longer necessary to the organism. But an organ never takes on a function that does not accord with its proper purpose.

The same is true of social institutions. They, too, do not arise arbitrarily, but are called into being by special social needs to serve definite purposes. In this way the modern state was evolved after monopoly economy, and the class divisions associated with it, had begun to make themselves more and more conspicuous in the framework of the old social order. The newly arisen possessing classes had need of a political instrument of power to maintain their economic and social privileges over the masses of their own people, and to impose them from without on other groups of human beings. Thus arose the appropriate social conditions for the evolution of the modern state, as the organ of political power of privileged castes and classes for the forcible subjugation and oppression of the non-possessing classes. This task is the political lifework of the state, the essential reason for its existing at all. And to this task it has always remained faithful, must remain faithful, for it cannot escape from its skin.

Its external forms have altered in the course of its historical development, but its functions have always remained the same. They have even been constantly broadened in just the measure in which its supporters have succeeded in making further fields of social activity subservient to their ends. Whether the state be monarchy or republic, whether historically it is anchored in an autocracy or in a national constitution, its function remains always the same. And just as the functions of the bodily organs of plants and animals cannot be arbitrarily altered, so that, for example, one cannot at will hear with his eyes and see with his ears, so also one cannot at pleasure transform an organ of social oppression into an instrument for the liberation of the oppressed. The state can only be what it is : the defender of mass-exploitation and social privileges, the creator of privileged classes and castes and of new monopolies. Who fails to

recognize this function of the state does not understand
the real nature of the present social order at all, and is
incapable of pointing out to humanity new outlooks for
its social evolution.

Anarchism is no patent solution for all human problems,
no Utopia of a perfect social order, as it has so often been
called, since on principle it rejects all absolute schemes
and concepts. It does not believe in any absolute
truth, or in definite final goals for human development,
but in an unlimited perfectibility of social arrangements
and human living conditions, which are always straining
after higher forms of expression, and to which for this
reason one can assign no definite terminus nor set any
fixed goal. The worst crime of every type of state is
just that it always tries to force the rich diversity of social
life into definite forms and adjust it to one particular
form, which allows for no wider outlook and regards the
previously exciting status as finished. The stronger its
supporters feel themselves, the more completely they
succeed in bringing every field of social life into their
service, the more crippling is their influence on the
operation of all creative cultural forces, the more unwholesomely does it affect the intellectual and social
development of any particular epoch.

The so-called totalitarian state, which now rests like
a mountain-weight upon whole peoples and tries to
mould every expression of their intellectual and social
life to the lifeless pattern set by a political providence,
suppresses with ruthless and brutal force every effort at
alteration of the existing conditions. The totalitarian
state is a dire omen for our time, and shows with frightful
clarity whither such a return to the barbarism of past
centuries must lead. It is the triumph of the political
machine over mind, the rationalizing of human thought,

feeling, and behaviour according to the established rules of the officials. It is consequently the end of all truly intellectual culture.

Anarchism recognizes only the relative significance of ideas, institutions, and social forms. It is, therefore, not a fixed, self-enclosed social system, but rather a definite trend in the historic development of mankind, which, in contrast with the intellectual guardianship of all clerical and governmental institutions, strives for the free unhindered unfolding of all the individual and social forces in life. Even freedom is only a relative, not an absolute concept, since it tends constantly to become broader and to affect wider circles in more manifold ways. For the Anarchist, freedom is not an abstract philosophical concept, but the vital concrete possibility for every human being to bring to full development all the powers, capacities, and talents with which nature has endowed him, and turn them to social account. The less this natural development of man is influenced by ecclesiastical or political guardianship, the more efficient and harmonious will human personality become, the more will it become the measure of the intellectual culture of the society in which it has grown.

This is the reason why all great culture periods in history have been periods of political weakness. And that is quite natural, for political systems are always set upon the mechanizing and not upon the organic development of social forces. State and culture are in the depth of their being irreconcilable opposites. Nietzsche recognized this very clearly when he wrote :

" No one can finally spend more than he has. That holds good for individuals ; it holds good for peoples. If one spends oneself for power, for high politics, for husbandry, for commerce, parliamentarism,

military .interests—if one gives away that amount of
reason, earnestness, will, self-mastery, which constitutes one's real self for one thing, he will not have
it for the other.   Culture and the state—let no one be
deceived about this—are antagonists : the ' Culture
State ' is merely a modern idea.   The one lives on the
other, the one prospers at the expense of the other.
All great periods of culture are periods of political
decline.   Whatever is great in a cultured sense is non-
political, is even anti-political."

A powerful state mechanism is the greatest hindrance
to any higher cultural development.   Where the state has
been attacked by internal decay, where the influence of
political power on the creative forces in society is reduced
to a minimum, there culture thrives best, for political
rulership always strives for uniformity and tends to
subject every aspect of social life to its guardianship.
And in this it finds itself in unescapable contradiction to
the creative aspirations of cultural development, which
is always on the quest after new forms and fields of social
activity, and for which freedom of expression, the many-
sidedness and the kaleidoscopic changes of things, are
just as vitally necessary as rigid forms, dead rules, and
the forcible suppression of every manifestation of social
life which are in contradiction to it.
    Every culture, if its natural development is not too
much affected by political restrictions, experiences a
perpetual renewal of the formative urge, and out of that
comes an ever growing diversity of creative activity.
Every successful piece of work stirs the desire for greater
perfection and deeper inspiration ; each new form
becomes the herald of new possibilities of development.
But the state creates no culture, as is so often thoughtlessly
asserted, it only tries to keep things as they are, safely

anchored to stereotypes. That has been the reason for all revolutions in history.

Power operates only destructively, bent always on forcing every manifestation of life into the straitjacket of its laws. Its intellectual form of expression is dead dogma, its physical form brute force. And this un-intelligence of its objectives sets its stamp on its supporters also and renders them stupid and brutal, even when they were originally endowed with the best of talents. One who is constantly striving to force everything into a mechanical order at last becomes a machine himself and loses all human feeling.

It was from the understanding of this that modern Anarchism was born and now draws its moral force. Only freedom can inspire men to great things and bring about intellectual and social transformations. The art of ruling men has never been the art of educating men and inspiring them to a new shaping of their lives. Dreary compulsion has at its command only lifeless drill, which smothers any vital initiative at its birth and can bring forth only subjects, not free men. Freedom is the very essence of life, the impelling force in all intellectual and social development, the creator of every new outlook for the future of mankind. The liberation of man from economic exploitation and from intellectual and political oppression, which finds its finest expression in the world-philosophy of Anarchism, is the first prerequisite for the evolution of a higher social culture and a new humanity.

2

THE PROLETARIAT AND THE BEGINNING OF
THE MODERN LABOUR MOVEMENT

The era of machine production and modern Capitalism ;
The rise of the Proletariat ; The first labour unions and
their struggle for existence ; Luddism ; Trade Unionism
pure and simple ; Political radicalism and labour ; the
Chartist movement ; Socialism and the labour movement.

MODERN Socialism was at first only a profounder understanding of the interconnections in social life, an attempt
to solve the contradictions implicit in the present social
order and to give a new content to man's relations with
his social environment. Its influence was, therefore, for
a time confined to a little circle of intellectuals, who for
the most part came from the privileged classes. Inspired
with a profound and noble sympathy for the material
and intellectual needs of the great masses they sought a
way out of the labyrinth of social antagonisms in order
to open to mankind new outlooks for its future development. For them Socialism was a cultural question ;
therefore, they made their appeal directly and chiefly
to the reason and ethical sense of their contemporaries,
hoping to find them receptive to the new insights.

But ideas do not make a movement ; they are themselves merely the product of concrete situations, the
intellectual precipitate of particular conditions of life.
Movements arise only from the immediate and practical

necessities of social life, and are never the result of purely abstract ideas. But they acquire their irresistible force and their inner certainty of victory only when they are vitalized by a great idea, which gives them life and intellectual content. It is only when viewed thus that the relation of the labour movement to Socialism can be correctly understood and intelligently valued. Socialism is not the creator of the modern labour movement; rather, it grew out of it. The movement developed as the logical result of a social reconstruction out of which the present capitalist world was born. Its immediate purpose was the struggle for daily bread, the conscious resistance to a trend of things which was constantly becoming more ruinous for the workers.

The modern labour movement owes its existence to the great industrial revolution which was going on in England in the latter half of the eighteenth century, and which has since then overflowed into all five continents. After the system of so-called " manufactures " had at an earlier period opened the road for a certain degree of division of labour—a division which was, however, concerned more with the methods of applying human labour than with actual technical processes—the great inventions of the subsequent period brought about a complete transformation of all the apparatus of work; the machine conquered the individual tool and created totally new forms for productive processes in general. The invention of the mechanical loom revolutionized the whole textile industry, the most important industry in England, and led to a complete new set of methods in the processing and dyeing of wool and cotton.

Through the utilization of steam power, made available by the epoch-making invention of James Watt, machine production was freed from its dependence on

the old motive forces of wind, water, and horse power,
and the way first properly opened for modern mass
production. The use of steam made possible the operation of machines of different function in the same rooms.
Thus arose the modern factory, which in a few decades
had shoved the small shop to the brink of the abyss.
This happened first in the textile industry ; the other
branches of production followed at short intervals. The
utilization of the power of steam and the invention of
cast steel led in a short time to a complete revolutionizing
of the iron and coal industries and rapidly extended their
influence to other lines of work. The development of
modern big plants had as a result the fabulous growth
of the industrial cities. Birmingham, which in 1801
boasted only 73,000 inhabitants, had in 1844 a population
of 200,000. Sheffield in the same period grew from
46,000 to 110,000. Other centres of the new big industries grew in the same ratio.

The factories needed human fodder, and the increasingly
impoverished rural population met the demand by
streaming into the cities. The legislature helped, when,
by the notorious *Enclosure Acts*, it robbed the small
farmers of the common lands and brought them to
beggary. The systematic theft of the commons had
already begun under Queen Anne (1702-1714), and by
1844 had taken in more than one-third of the tillable
land of England and Wales. While in 1786 there had
still existed 250,000 independent landowners, in the
course of only thirty years their number had been reduced
to 32,000.

The new machine production increased the so-called
national wealth on an undreamed-of scale. But this
wealth was in the hands of a small privileged minority
and owed its origin to the unrestrained exploitation of the

working population, which by the rapid alteration of the economic conditions of living was plunged into the most revolting misery. If one reads the dismal description of the situation of the workers of that period as it is set down in the reports of the English factory inspectors, of which Marx made such effective use in his *Capital ;* or if one picks up a book like Eugene Buret's *De la misère des classes labeurieuses en Angleterre et France*, to which Friedrich Engels was so deeply indebted in his initial work, *The Conditions of the Working Classes in England ;* or any one of numerous works by contemporary English authors, one gets a picture of that time which staggers the mind.

If Arthur Young, in his well-known account of his travels in France just before the outbreak of the Great Revolution, could declare that a large part of the French rural population stood almost on the level of beasts, having lost every trace of humanity as a result of their horrible poverty, the comparison could apply in large measure also to the intellectual and material status of the great masses of the rising industrial proletariat in the initial period of modern capitalism.

The enormous majority of the workers dwelt in miserable dirty holes without even a glass window, and they had to spend from fourteen to fifteen hours a day in the sweatshops of industry, innocent of either hygienic equipment or provision for the protection of the lives and health of the inmates. And this for a wage that was never enough to satisfy even the most indispensable needs. If at the end of the week the worker had enough left to enable him to forget the hell he lived in for a few hours by getting drunk on bad liquor, it was the most he could achieve. The inevitable consequence of such a state of affairs was an enormous increase in prostitution,

drunkenness, and crime. The utter wretchedness of
mankind dawns on one when he reads of the spiritual
degradation and moral depravity of those masses whom
no one pitied.

The pitiful situation of the factory slaves was made
still more oppressive by the so-called truck system, under
which the worker was compelled to purchase his provisions and other articles of daily use in the stores of the
factory-owners, where often over-priced and unusable
goods were handed out to him. This went so far that
the workers had scarcely anything left of their hard-
earned wages, and had to pay for unexpected expenses,
such as doctors, medicines, and the like, with the goods
they had received from the factory owners, which they
had, of course, to turn in in such cases at a lower price
than they had been charged for them. And contemporary
writers tell how mothers, in order to provide burial for
a dead child, would have to pay the undertaker and the
gravedigger in this way.

And this limitless exploitation of human labour power
was not confined to men and women. The new methods
of work had enabled the machine to be served with just
a few manual movements, which could be learned with
no great difficulty. This led to the destruction of the
children of the proletariat, who were put to work at the
age of three or four years and had to drag out their
youth in the industrial prisons of the entrepreneurs.
The story of child labour, on which no legal restrictions
of any kind were imposed at first, is one of the darkest
chapters in the history of capitalism. It shows to what
lengths of heartlessness a Christian management would
go, untroubled by ethical considerations, and unthink-
ingly accustomed to unrestricted exploitation of the
masses. Prolonged labour under the unwholesome

conditions of the factories at last raised child mortality to a point where Richard Carlile could, with perfect justice, speak of a " gruesome repetition on a larger scale of the slaughter of the innocents at Bethlehem." Not until then did parliament enact laws for the protection of child labour, laws which were for a long time evaded by the factory owners, or simply broken.

The state lent its best assistance to the freeing of management from restrictions burdensome on its lust for exploitation. It provided it with cheap labour. For this purpose, for example, there was devised the notorious Poor Law of 1834, which roused such a storm of indignation, not only from the English working class, but from everyone who still carried a heart in his bosom. The old Poor Law, which had originated in 1601, under Queen Elizabeth, was an outcome of the suppression of the monasteries in England. The monasteries had made a practice of expending a third of their income on the maintenance of the poor. But the noble proprietors to whom the greater part of the monastic holdings had fallen, had no thought of continuing to devote the required third to alms, so the law imposed on the parishes the duty of caring for their poor and finding some human means of subsistence for those whose existence had been uprooted. The law saw in poverty a personal misfortune for which the human being was not responsible, and conceded to him the right to call upon society for aid when through no fault of his own he had fallen into need and was no longer able to provide for himself. This natural consideration gave the law a social character.

The new law, however, branded poverty as a crime, and laid the responsibility for personal misfortune upon alleged indolence. The new law had been brought into existence under the fateful influence of the Malthusian doctrine, whose misanthropic teachings had been hailed by the possessing classes as a new revelation. Malthus, whose well-known work on the population problem had been conceived as an answer to Godwin's *Political Justice*, had announced in blunt words that the poor man forced his way into society as an uninvited guest, and could therefore lay no claim to special rights or to the pity of his fellow men. Such a view was, of course, grist to the mill of the industrial barons and gave the required moral support to their unlimited lust for exploitation.

The new law took the provision for the maintenance of the poor out of the hands of the parish authorities and put it under a central body appointed by the state. Material support by money or provisions was for the most part abolished, and replaced by the so-called work-house, that notorious and hated institution which in the popular speech was called the "poor law Bastille." He who, smitten by fate, was compelled to seek refuge in the workhouse, surrendered his status as a human being, for these houses were outright prisons, in which the individual was punished and humiliated for his personal misfortune. In the workhouses an iron discipline prevailed, which countered any opposition with strict punishment. Everyone had a definite task to perform ; anyone who was not able to do it was deprived of food in punishment. The food was worse and more inadequate than in actual prisons, and the treatment so harsh and barbarous that children were often driven to suicide. Families were separated and their members permitted to see one another only at stated times and under the supervision of the officials. Every effort was directed to making residence in this place of terror so unendurable that only the utmost necessity would drive human beings to seek in it a last refuge. For that was the real purpose of the new poor law. Machine production had driven thousands out of their old means of living—in the textile industries alone more than 80,000 hand weavers had been made beggars by the modern big plants—and the new law saw to it that cheap labour was at the command of management, and with it the possibility of constantly forcing wages lower.

Under these horrible conditions a new social class was born, which had no forerunners in history : the modern industrial proletariat. The small craftsman of former times, who served principally the local demand, enjoyed comparatively satisfactory living conditions, which were only rarely disturbed by any considerable shock from without. He served his apprenticeship, became a journeyman, and often, later, a master himself, as the acquisition of the necessary tools of his trade was not dependent on the possession of any great amount of capital, as it became in the era of the machine. His work was worthy of a human being and still offered that natural variety which incites to creative activity and guarantees inner satisfaction to man.

Even the small home industrialist, who at the beginning of the capitalist era was already disposing of the greater part of his product to the rich lords of trade in the cities, was far from being a proletarian in the present sense. Industry, the textile industry in particular, had its centres in the rural districts, so that the small craftsmen in most instances had at his disposal a tiny bit of land, which made maintenance easier for him. And as the oncoming capitalism was, before the domination of the machine, still tied to the handicraft stage of industry, its possibilities of expansion were for the time limited, since the demand for the products of industry was as a rule greater

than the supply, so that the worker was safeguarded
against serious economic crises.

However, all that was changed within a very few years
after modern machine production had began to play its
part, as it was dependent in advance on mass demand,
and hence on the conquest of foreign markets. Each
new invention raised the capacity for production in ever
increasing measure and made industrial capital the
undisputed master of capitalist industry, dominating
trade and finance. And since free competition, which
was held by the theorists to be an iron economic law,
put any planned control of industrial production out of
the question, at longer or shorter intervals there must
occur periods when, owing to various causes, the supply
of industrial products outstripped the demand. This
brought on abrupt cessations of production, so-called
crises, which were ruinous to the proletarian population
of the cities because they condemned the workers to
enforced inactivity and so deprived them of the means of
living. It is just this phenomenon of so-called " over-
production," which is so indicative of the real nature of
modern capitalism—this condition in which, while
factories and warehouses are crammed with wares, the
actual producers are languishing in bitterest misery.
It is this which reveals most plainly the horror of a system
for which man is nothing and dead possessions are
everything.

But the developing proletariat was completely exposed
to the economic fluctuations of this system, since its
members had nothing to dispose of except the labour of
their hands. The natural human ties which existed
between the old master-workman and his journeymen
had no meaning for the modern proletarian. He was
merely the object of exploitation by a class with which

he no longer had any social relationship. For the factory owner he existed merely as a " hand," not any more as a human being. He was, one might say, the chaff which the great industrial revolution of that time had swept up in heaps in the cities, after he had lost all social standing. Socially uprooted, he had become just a component of a great mass of shipwrecked beings, who had all been smitten by the same fate. The modern proletarian, he was the man of the machine, a machine of flesh and blood who set the machine of steel in motion, to create wealth for others, while the actual producer of this wealth must perish in misery.

And dwelling close-packed with his comrades-in-misfortune in the great centres of industry not only gave a peculiar character to his material existence, it also gradually created for his thinking and feeling new concepts which he had not originally known. Transplanted into a new world of pounding machines and reeking chimneys, he at first felt himself merely as a wheel or a cog in a mighty mechanism against which he as an individual was helpless. He dared not even hope sooner or later to escape from this condition, since to him, as the typical dispossessed with no means of keeping alive except by the sale of his hands, every way out was barred. And not he alone, his posterity as well was doomed to the same fate. Bereft of every social tie, he was personally a mere nothing in comparison with that enormous power which was using him as the insensate tool of its selfish interests. In order to become something once more and to effect some betterment of his lot, he would have to act along with others of his kind and call a halt to the fate that had smitten him. Such considerations had sooner or later to control him if he did not wish simply to sink into the abyss ; they led to the formation of the

first proletarian alliances to the modern labour movement as a whole.

It was not the " agitator " who conjured this movement
of the dispossessed masses into life, as narrow-minded
reactionaries and a rapacious management dared to
assert then, and still assert even to-day ; it was the
conditions themselves which roused to life the movement and with it its spokesmen. The combination of
the workers was the only means at their command for
saving their lives and forcing more human conditions
under which to live. The first proposals of these bands
of organized wage-workers, which can be traced back to
the first half of the eighteenth century, went no further
than the abolition of the most crying evils of the capitalist
system and some improvement of the existing conditions
of living.

Since 1350 there had existed in England a statute in
accordance with which apprenticeship, wages, and hours
were regulated by the state. The alliances of the ancient
craft corporations concerned themselves only with
questions relating to the production of commodities
and the right of disposal of them. But when, with
incipient capitalism, and the spread of " manufactures,"
wages began to be pushed down further and further,
the first trade union organizations developed among
the new class of wage-workers to combat this tendency.
But these efforts of the organized workers at once en-
countered the unanimous resistance of the managers,
who besieged the government with petitions to uphold
the ancient law and to suppress the " unlawful " organizations of the workers. And parliament promptly responded to this demand by passing the so-called Combination Acts of 1799-1800, which prohibited all combinations for the purpose of raising wages or improving

the existing conditions of work and imposed severe penalties for violation.

Thus labour was given over unconditionally to exploitation by industrial capital, and was faced with the alternatives of, either submitting to the law and accepting without resistance all the consequences this entailed, or breaking the law which had condemned them to outright slavery. Confronted with such a choice the decision could not have been too difficult for the more courageous section of the workers, as they had scarcely anything more to lose any way. They defied the law which mocked at human dignity, and tried by every means to get around its provisions. Since the trade union organizations, which were at first purely local in character and confined to particular industries, had been deprived of the legal right to exist, there sprang up all over the country so-called mutual benefit associations or similar innocuous bodies, having as their sole purpose the diverting of attention from the actual fighting organizations of the proletarians.

For the inner core of these open associations was composed of the secret conspiratory brotherhoods of the militant element among the workers, smaller or larger groups of determined men, bound by an oath to profoundest secrecy and mutual assistance. In the northern industrial sections of England and in Scotland in particular there were a large number of these secret organizations, which carried on the fight against the employers and spurred the workers to resistance. It lay in the nature of the affair that most of these struggles assumed an extremely violent character, as is easy to understand when we consider the miserable situation of the workers resulting from the disastrous development of economic conditions and the pitiless prosecutions following even the

most modest attempt at improvement of the proletarian
standard of living. Any violation of the letter of the
law was visited with horrible punishment. Even after
trade union organizations were legally recognized in
1824, the prosecutions did not cease for a long time.
Conscienceless judges, openly and cynically protecting
the class interests of the employers, inflicted hundreds
of years of imprisonment on insubordinate workers, and
a considerable time elapsed before somewhat endurable
conditions prevailed.

In 1812, the secret labour organizations brought about
a general strike of the weavers in Glasgow. In the
following years the whole of Northern England was
continually shaken by strikes and unrest among the
workers, which finally culminated in the great strike of
the weavers and spinners in Lancashire in 1818, in which
the workers, in addition to the usual demand for better
wages, called for reform of factory legislation and humane
regulation of the labour of women and children. The
same year brought the great strike of the Scotch miners,
which was staged by their secret organizations. In the
same way the greater part of the Scottish textile industry
was periodically crippled by cessation of labour. Often
the strikes were accompanied by arson, destruction of
property, and public disorder, so that the government
was frequently under the necessity of throwing the
militia into the industrial sections.

As later in every other country, so then in England,
the resentment of the workers was directed against the
introduction of the machines, the social importance of
which they did not yet recognize, and which were the
immediate cause of their want. As early as 1769, a
special law had been enacted for the protection of the
machines ; but later, when the application of steam power

started a rapid advance in machine production, and, in
the textile industry in particular, thousands of hand-
workers were robbed of the means of subsistence and
plunged into deepest misery, the destruction of machines
became an everyday occurrence. This was the period of
so-called Luddism. In 1811, over two hundred machine
looms were destroyed in Nottingham. In Arnold,
where the introduction of stocking-weaving machinery
had thrown hundreds of the old stocking-weavers on
the pavement, the workers stormed the factories and
demolished sixty of the new machines, each of which
represented an investment of forty pounds. Similar
performances were repeated everywhere.

What was the good of laws, so long as the need of the
proletarian population was steadily increasing, and
management and government had neither understanding
nor sympathy for their situation ! *King Ludd*[1] made
his royal entry in industrial circles everywhere, and even
the harshest laws were unable to put a stop to his work of
destruction. " Stop him who dares ; stop him who can ! "
was the watchword of the secret workers' societies.
The destruction of the machines ceased only when a
new understanding of the matter arose among the workers
themselves, and they came to see that they could not halt
technical progress by this means.

In 1812, parliament enacted a law imposing the death
penalty for the destruction of machines. It was on this
occasion that Lord Byron delivered his celebrated indict-
ment of the government and ironically demanded that,
if the bloody law was to be put in force, the house should

[1] The origin of the word is veiled in darkness. Some trace it to
a weaver by the name of Ned Ludd, but there is no historical basis
for this. In some regions they talked of " Jack Swing " and
" Great Enoch," but the meaning of all the names was the
same.

provide that the jury should always consist of twelve butchers.[1]

The officials put a price of forty thousand pounds on the heads of the leaders of the underground movement. In January of 1813, eighteen workers convicted of Luddism were hanged at York, and the deportation of organized workers to the penal colonies in Australia increased at a frightful rate. But the movement itself only grew the faster, particularly when the great business crisis set in after the end of the Napoleonic wars, and the discharged soldiers and sailors were added to the army of the unemployed. This situation was made still tenser by several short harvests and the notorious corn laws of 1815, by which the price of bread was raised artificially.

But although this first phase of the modern labour movement was in great part a violent one, it still was not revolutionary in the proper sense. For this it lacked that deeper understanding of the actual causes of economic and social processes which only Socialism could give it. Its violent methods were merely the result of the brutal violence which was inflicted on the workers themselves. But the efforts of the young movement were not directed against the capitalist system as such at all, but merely at the abolishment of its most pernicious excrescences and at the establishment of a descent human standard of living for the proletariat. " A fair day's wage for a fair day's work " was the slogan of these first unions, and when the employers resisted this modest and certainly fully justified demand of the workers with the

[1] Lord Byron felt a strong sympathy for the Luddites, as is shown by one of his poems, the first stanza of which runs :

> " As the Liberty lads o'er the sea
> Bought their freedom, and cheaply, with blood,
> So we, boys, we
> Will die fighting, or live free,
> And down with all kings but King Ludd ! "

utmost brutality, the latter were obliged to resort to whatever methods were available to them under the existing conditions.

The great historical significance of the movement lay at first less in its actual social objectives than in its simple existence. It gave a footing once more to the uprooted masses which the pressure of economic conditions had driven into the great industrial centres. It revived their social sense. The class struggle against the exploiters awakened the solidarity of the workers and gave new meaning to their lives. It breathed new hope into the victims of an economy of unrestricted exploitation and showed them a course which offered the possibility of safeguarding their lives and defending their outraged human dignity. It strengthened the workers' self-reliance and gave them confidence in the future once more. It trained the workers in self-discipline and organized resistance, and developed in them the consciousness of their strength and their importance as a social factor in the life of their time. This was the great moral service of that movement which was born of the necessities of the situation, and which only he can undervalue who is blind to social problems and without sympathy for the sufferings of his fellow men.

When, then, in 1824, the laws against the combination of workers were repealed, when the government and that section of the middle class possessed of insight had at last become convinced that even the harshest prosecution would never break up the movement, the trade union organization of the workers spread over the entire country at an undreamed-of rate. The earlier local groups combined into larger unions and thus gave to the movement its real importance. Even the reactionary turns in the government were no longer able to control this development. They merely increased the number of victims among its adherents, but they could not turn back the movement itself.

The new upsurge of political radicalism in England after the long French wars naturally had a strong influence on the English working class also. Men like Burdett, Henry Hunt, Major Cartwright, and above all William Cobbett, whose paper the *Political Register*, after the price had been reduced to twopence, attained a circulation of sixty thousand, were the intellectual heads of the new reform movement. This was directing its attacks chiefly against the corn laws, the Combination Acts of 1799-1800, and, most of all, against the corrupt electoral system under which even a large part of the middle class was excluded from the franchise. Huge mass meetings in every section of the country, and particularly in the northern industrial districts, set the populace in motion. But the reactionary government under Castlereagh opposed any reform, and was determined from the first to put an end to the reform movement by force. When in August, 1819, sixty thousand people poured into the Petersfield in Manchester to formulate a mass petition to the government, the assembly was dispersed by the militia, and four hundred persons were wounded or killed.

To the stormy outburst in the country against the instigators of the massacre of " Peterloo " the government replied with the notorious six gag laws, by which the right of assembly and freedom of the press were in effect suspended and the reformers made liable to the harshest prosecution. By the so-called " Cato Street Conspiracy," in which Arthur Thistlewood and his associates planned the assassination of the members of the British Cabinet, the government was given the wished for opportunity to proceed with draconic severity against the reform movement. On May 1, 1820, Thistlewood and four of his comrades paid for their attempt on the gallows : the *habeas corpus* act was suspended for two years, and England was delivered to a reactionary regime which respected none of the rights of its citizens.

This put a stop to the movement for the time being. Then the July revolution of 1830 in France led to a revival of the English reform movement, which, this time, took on an entirely different character. The fight for parliamentary reform flared up anew. But after the bourgeoisie saw the greater part of their demands satisfied by the Reform Bill of 1832, a victory which they owned only to the energetic support of the workers, they opposed all further attempts at reform, looking towards universal suffrage, and left the workers to depart empty-handed. Not only that : the new parliament enacted a number of reactionary laws by which the workers' right to organize was again seriously threatened. The shining examples among these new laws were the notorious poor laws of 1834, to which reference had already been made. The workers felt that they had been sold and betrayed, and this feeling led to a complete break with the middle class.

The new reform movement from now on found vigorous expression in the developing Chartism, which, it is true, was supported by a considerable part of the petty bourgeoisie, but in which the proletarian element everywhere took an energetic part. Chartism, of course, had inscribed on its banner the celebrated six points of the charter, which aimed at radical parliamentary reform, but it had also appropriated all the social demands of the workers and was trying by every form of direct attack to transform these into realities. Thus J. R. Stephens, one of the most influential leaders of the Chartist movement,

declared before a great mass meeting in Manchester
that Chartism was not a political question which would
be settled by the introduction of universal suffrage,
but was instead to be regarded as a " bread and butter
question," since the charter would mean good homes,
abundant food, human associations, and short hours
of labour for the workers. It was for this reason that
propaganda for the celebrated Ten-hour Bill played
such an important part in the movement.

With the Chartist movement England had entered upon
a revolutionary period, and wide circles of both the bourgeoisie and the working class were convinced that a civil
war was close at hand. Huge mass meetings in every
section of the country testified to the rapid spread of
the movement, and numerous strikes and constant unrest
among the workers in the cities gave it a threatening
aspect. The frightened employers organized numerous
armed leagues " for the protection of persons and property " in the industrial centres. This led to the workers
also beginning to arm. By a resolution of the Chartist
convention, which convened in London in March of
1839, and was later moved to Birmingham, fifteen of
their best orators were sent out to every section of the
country to make the people acquainted with the aims of
the movement and to collect signatures to the Chartist
petition. Their meetings were attended by hundreds of
thousands, and showed what a response the movement
had aroused among the masses of the people.

Chartism had a large number of intelligent and self-
sacrificing spokesmen, such as William Lovell, Feargus
O'Connor, Branterre O'Brien, J. R. Stephens, Henry
Hetherington, James Watson, Henry Vincent, John
Taylor, A. H. Beaumont, Ernest Jones, to mention only
a few of the best known. It commanded, in addition, a

fairly widespread press, of which papers like *The Poor Man's Guardian* and the *Northern Star* exerted the greatest influence. Chartism was, as a matter of fact, not a movement with definite aims, but rather a catchbasin for the social discontent of the time, but it did effect a shaking-up, especially of the working class, whom it made receptive to far-reaching social aims. Socialism also forged vigorously ahead during the Chartist period, and the ideas of William Thompson, John Gray, and especially of Robert Owen, began to spread more widely among the English workers.

In France, Belgium, and the Rhine country also, where industrial capitalism first established itself on the Continent, it was everywhere accompanied by the same phenomena and led, of necessity, to the initial stages of a labour movement. And this movement manifested itself at first in every country in the same primitive form, which only gradually yielded to a better understanding, until at last its permeation by Socialist ideas endowed it with loftier conceptions and opened for it new social outlooks. The alliance of the labour movement with Socialism was of decisive importance for both. But the political ideas which influenced this, that, or the other Socialist school determined the character of the movement in each instance, and its outlook for the future as well.

While certain schools of Socialism remained quite indifferent or unsympathetic to the young labour movement, others of them quickly recognized the real importance of this movement as the necessary preliminary to the realization of Socialism. They understood that it must be their task to take an active part in the every day struggles of the workers, so as to make clear to the toiling masses the intimate connection between their immediate demands and the Socialist objectives. For these struggles, growing out of the needs of the moment, serve to bring about a correct understanding of the profound importance of the liberation of the proletariat for the complete suppression of wage slavery. Although sprung from the immediate necessities of life, the movement, nevertheless, bore within it the germ of things to come, and these were to set new goals for life. Everything new arises from the realities of vital being. New worlds are not born in the vacuum of abstract ideas, but in the fight for daily bread, in that hard and ceaseless struggle which the needs and worries of the hour demand just to take care of the indispensable requirements of life. In the constant warfare against the already existing, the new shapes itself and comes to fruition. He who does not know how to value the achievements of the hour will never be able to conquer a better future for himself and his fellows.

From their daily battles against the employers and their allies, the workers gradually learn the deeper meaning of this struggle. At first they pursue only the immediate purpose of improving the status of the producers within the existing social order, but gradually they lay bare the root of the evil—monopoly economy and its political and social accompaniments. For the attainment of such an understanding the every day struggles are better educative material than the finest theoretical discussions. Nothing can so impress the mind and soul of the worker as this enduring battle for daily bread, nothing makes him so receptive to the teachings of Socialism as the incessant struggle for the necessities of life.

Just as in the time of feudal dominion the bondsmen peasants by their frequent uprisings—which had at first only the purpose of wresting from the feudal lords certain concessions which would mean some betterment of their dreary standard of living—prepared the way for the Great Revolution by which the abolition of feudal privileges was practically brought about ; so the innumerable labour wars within capitalist society constitute, one might say, the introduction to that great social revolution of the future which shall make Socialism a living reality. Without the incessant revolts of the peasantry—Taine reports that between 1781 and the storming of the Bastille nearly five hundred of these revolts occurred in almost every part of France—the idea of the perniciousness of the whole system of serfdom and feudalism would never have entered the heads of the masses.

That is just how it stands with the economic and social struggles of the modern working class. It would be utterly wrong to estimate these merely on the basis of their material origin or their practical results and to overlook their deeper psychologic significance. Only from the every day conflicts between labour and capital could the doctrines of Socialism, which had arisen in the minds of individual thinkers, take on flesh and blood and acquire that peculiar character which make of them a mass movement, the embodiment of a new cultural ideal for the future.

3

THE FORERUNNERS OF SYNDICALISM

Robert Owen and the English labour movement ; The Grand National Consolidated Trade Union ; William Benbow and the idea of the General Strike ; The period of reaction ; Evolution of the labour organizations in France ; The International Workingmen's Association ; The new conception of trade unionism ; The idea of the labour councils ; Labour councils versus dictatorships ; Bakunin on the economic organization of the workers ; The introduction of parliamentary politics by Marx and Engels and the end of the International.

THE permeation of the labour movement by Socialist ideas early led to tendencies which had an unmistakable relationship to the revolutionary Syndicalism of our day. These tendencies developed first in England, the mother country of capitalist big industry, and for a time strongly influenced the advanced sections of the English working class. After the repeal of the Combination Acts, the effort of the workers was directed chiefly to giving a broader character to their trade union organizations, as practical experience had shown them that purely local organizations could not provide the needed support in their struggles for daily bread. Still these efforts were not at first based on any very profound social concepts. The workers, except in so far as they were influenced by the political reform movement of that time, had no goal whatever in view outside the immediate betterment of their economic status. Not until the beginning of the 30's did the influence of Socialist ideas on the English labour movement become plainly apparent, and its appearance then is to be ascribed chiefly to the stirring propaganda of Robert Owen and his followers.

A few years before the convening of the so-called Reform Parliament the *National Union of the Working Classes* was founded, its most important component part being the workers in the textile industries. This combination had summed up its demands in the following four points : 1. To every worker the full value of his labour. 2. Protection of the workers against the employers by every appropriate means, which means will develop automatically out of the current conditions. 3. The reform of parliament and universal suffrage for both men and women. 4. Education of workers in economic problems. One recognizes in these demands the strong influence of the political reform movement which just at that time held the entire country under its spell ; but at the same time one notices expressions which are borrowed from the doctrines of Robert Owen.

The year 1832 brought the Reform Bill, by which the last political illusions for large circles of the English working class were destroyed. When the bill had become law it was seen that the middle class had, indeed, won a great victory over the aristocratic landowners, but the workers recognized that they had been betrayed again, and that they had merely been used by the bourgeoisie to pull its chestnuts out of the fire. The result was a general disillusionment and the steadily spreading conviction that the working class could find no help in an alliance with the bourgeoisie. If, before then, the class struggle had been an actuality which arose spontaneously out of the conflicting economic interests of the possessing and non-possessing classes, it had now taken shape as a definite conviction in the minds of the workers and gave a determinate course to their activities. This turn in the thinking of the working class is clearly revealed in numerous utterances in the labour press during those years. The workers were beginning to understand that their real strength lay in their character as producers. The more keenly aware they became of the fiasco of their participation in the political reform movement, the more firmly rooted became their newly acquired understanding of their own economic importance in society.

They were strengthened in this conviction in high degree by the propaganda of Robert Owen, who at that time was gaining constantly stronger influence in the ranks of organized labour. Owen recognized that the steady growth of trade union organizations furnished a firm basis for his efforts at a fundamental alteration of the capitalist economic order, and this filled him with high hopes. He showed the workers that the existing conflict between capital and labour could never be settled by ordinary battles over wages, though, in fact, he by no means overlooked the great importance of these to the workers. On the other hand he strove to convince the workers that they could expect nothing whatever from legislative bodies, and must take their affairs into their own hands. These ideas found willing ears among the advanced sections of the English working class, and first manifested themselves strongly among the building trades. The *Builders' Union*, in which were combined a considerable number of local labour unions, was at that time one of the most advanced and most active of labour organizations, and was a thorn in the flesh of the managers.

In the year 1831, Owen had presented his plans for the reconstruction of society before a meeting of delegates of this union in Manchester. The plans amounted to a kind of Guild Socialism and called for the establishment of producers' co-operatives under the control of the trade unions. The proposals were adopted, but shortly after this the Builders' Union was involved in a long series of severe conflicts, the unhappy outcome of which seriously threatened the existence of the organization and put a premature end to all efforts in the direction marked out by Owen.

Owen did not let himself be discouraged by this, but carried on his activities with renewed zeal. In 1833 there convened in London a conference of trade union and co-operative organizations, at which Owen explained exhaustively his plan for social reconstruction by the workers themselves. From the reports of the delegates one can see plainly what an influence these ideas had already gained and what a creative spirit then animated the advanced circles of the English working class. *The Poor Man's Guardian* very justly summed up its report of the conference in these words :

> " But far different from the paltry objects of all former combinations is that now aimed at by the congress of delegates. Their reports show that an entire change in society—a change amounting to a complete subversion of the existing order of the world —is contemplated by the working classes. They aspire to be at the top instead of the bottom of society —or rather that there should be no bottom or top at all."

The immediate result of this conference was the founding of the *Grand National Consolidated Trade Union of*

Great Britain and Ireland at the beginning of 1834.
Those were stirring times. The whole country was
shaken by innumerable strikes and lock-outs, and the
number of workers organized in trade unions rapidly
soared to 800,000. The founding of the G.N.C. arose
from the effort to gather the scattered organizations into
one great federation, which would give greater effective
force to the actions of the workers. But what distinguished this alliance from all the efforts in this direction
which had been made previously was that it stood, neither
for pure trades unionism, nor for collaboration of the
workers with the political reformers. The G.N.C. was
conceived as a fighting organization to lend all possible
aid to the workers in their daily struggle for the needed
betterment of their condition, but it had at the same time
set itself the goal of overthrowing capitalist economy as a
whole and replacing it with the co-operative labour of all
producers, which should no longer have in view profits
for individuals, but the satisfaction of the needs of all.
The G.N.C. was, then, to be the framework within which
these aspirations would find expression and be transformed into reality.

The organizers wanted to combine in these federations
the workers in all industrial and agricultural pursuits and
group them according to their special branches of production. Each industry would constitute a special
division which would concern itself with the special
conditions of their productive activity and the related
administrative functions. Wherever this was possible
the workers in the various branches of production were
to proceed to the establishment of co-operative plants,
which should sell their products to consumers at actual
cost, including the expense of administration. Universal
organization would serve to bind the separate industries

together organically and to regulate their mutual interests. The exchange of products of the co-operative plants was to be effected through so-called labour bazaars and the use of special exchange money or labour-tickets. By the steady spread of these institutions they hoped to drive capitalist competition from the field and thus to achieve a complete reorganization of society.

At the same time these co-operative agricultural and industrial undertakings were to serve to make the day-to-day struggles of the workers in the capitalist world easier. This is shown particularly in three of the seven points in which the G.N.C. had framed its demands :

" As land is the source of the first necessaries of life, and as, without the possession of it, the producing classes will ever remain in a greater or less degree subservient to the money capitalists, and subsequent upon the fluctuations of trade and commerce, this committee advises that a great effort should now be made by the unions to secure such portions of it on lease as their funds will permit, in order that in all turn-outs the men may be employed in rearing the greater part, if not the whole, of their subsistence under the direction of practical agricultural superintendents, which arrangements would not have the effect of lowering the price of labour in any trade, but on the contrary would rather tend to increase it by drawing off the at present superfluous supply in manufactures.

" The committee would, nevertheless, earnestly recommend in all cases of strikes and turn-outs, where it is practicable, that the men be employed in the making or producing of all such commodities as would be in demand among their brother unionists ; and that to effect this, each lodge should be provided with a workroom or shop in which those commodities may be manufactured on account of such lodge, which

shall make proper arrangements for the supply of the
necessary materials.

" That in all cases where it is practicable, each
district or branch should establish one or more depots
of provisions and articles in general domestic use : by
which means the working man may be supplied with
the best commodities at little above wholesale prices."

The G.N.C. was, therefore, conceived by its founders
as an alliance of trade unions and co-operatives. By his
practical participation in co-operative undertakings the
worker was to gain the understanding necessary for the
administration of the industry and thus be fitted to bring
ever wider circles of social production under their
control, until at last the whole economic life should be
conducted by the producers themselves and an end put to
all exploitation. These ideas found surprisingly clear
expression in workers' meetings and, more particularly,
in the labour press. If, for example, one reads *The
Pioneer*, the organ of the G.N.C. managed by James
Morrison, one frequently encounters arguments that
sound thoroughly modern. This is revealed especially
in the discussions with the political reformers, who had
inscribed on their banner the democratic reconstruction
of the House of Commons. They were told in reply
that the workers had no interest whatever in efforts of
that sort, since an economic transformation of society in
the Socialist sense would render the House of Commons
superfluous. Its place would be taken by the labour
boards and the industrial federations, which would
concern themselves merely with problems of production
and consumption in the interest of the people. These
organizations were destined to take over the functions
of the present entrepreneurs ; with common ownership
of all social wealth there would no longer be any need for

political institutions. The wealth of the nation would no longer be determined by the quantity of goods produced, but by the personal advantage that every individual derived from them. The House of Commons would in the future be merely a *House of Trades*.

The G.N.C. met with an extraordinary response from the workers. In a few months it embraced much over a half million members, and even though its actual aims were clearly understood at first only by the most intellectually active elements among the workers, still the great masses recognized, at least, that an organization of such dimensions could lend much greater weight to their demands than could local groups. The agitation for the ten-hour day had then taken firm hold on all sections of the English working class, and the G.N.C. set itself with all its energy to enforce this demand. Owen himself, and his close friends, Doherty, Fielden, and Grant, took a prominent part in this movement. However, the militants in the G.N.C. placed little hope in legislation, but tried to convince the workers that the ten-hour day could only be won by the united economic action of the whole body of workers. " The adults in factories must by unions among themselves make a *Short Time Bill* for themselves." This was their slogan.

The idea of the general strike met, at that time, with the undivided sympathy of the organized English workers. At the beginning of 1832, William Benbow, one of the most active champions of the new movement, had published a pamphlet entitled *Grand National Holiday and Congress of the Productive Classes*, which had a tremendous circulation, and in which the idea of the general strike and its importance to the working class was for the first time treated in its full compass. Benbow told the workers that if the enforced sale of their labour power was the cause of their slavery, then their organized refusal to work must be the means for their liberation. Such an instrument of warfare dispensed with any use of physical force and could achieve incomparably greater effects than the best army. All that was needed to bring about the downfall of the system of organized injustice was that the workers should grasp the importance of this powerful weapon and learn to use it with intelligence. Benbow advanced a lot of proposals, such as preparation for the general strike in the whole country by the establishment of local committees, so that the eruption might burst with elemental force, and his ideas at that time met with the heartiest response from the workers.

The rapid growth of the G.N.C. and, even more, the spirit that emanated from it, filled the employers with secret fear and blind hatred of the new combination. They felt that this movement must be stifled at the very outset before it had time to spread farther and build up and consolidate its local groups. The entire bourgeois press denounced the " criminal purposes " of the G.N.C., and unanimously proclaimed that it was leading the country toward a catastrophe. The factory owners in every industry besieged parliament with petitions urging measures against " unlawful combinations," and in particular against the collaboration of workers in different categories in industrial disputes. Many employers laid before their workers the so-called " document," and offered them the alternative of withdrawing from their unions or being thrown on the street by a lock-out.

Parliament did not, it is true, re-enact the old Combination Acts, but the government encouraged the judges to deal with the " excesses " of the workers as severely as they could within the framework of existing laws. And they did so in generous measure, being often able to use as a handle the fact that many unions had retained from the days of their underground activity before the repeal of the Combination Acts the formula of the oath and other ceremonial forms, and that this was contrary to the letter of the law. Hundreds of workers were sentenced to horrible punishments for the most trivial offences. Among the terrorist sentences of that time that imposed on six field hands in Dorchester aroused the bitterest indignation. Through the initiative of the G.N.C. the field workers in Tolpuddle, a little village near Dorchester, had formed a union and demanded an increase of wages from seven shillings to eight shillings a week. Shortly afterward six field hands were arrested and sentenced to the frightful penalty of transportation for seven years to the penal colonies in Australia. Their sole crime consisted in belonging to a union.

Thus from the very beginning the G.N.C. was involved in a long series of important wage wars and was subjected besides to constant and bitter prosecutions, so that it hardly found time to begin in earnest its great work of educating the masses. Perhaps, in any case, the time for that was not yet ripe. Many of its members turned to the awakening Chartism, which accepted many of its immediate demands, and along with other matters kept up the propaganda for the general strike, culminating in 1842 in that great movement which tied up all the industries of Lancashire, Yorkshire, Staffordshire, the Potteries, Wales, and the coal districts of Scotland. But the original significance of the movement had worn off, and Owen had been right when he accused Chartism of laying too much weight on political reform and showing too little understanding of the great economic problems. The unhappy revolutions of 1848-49 on the Continent led also to the decline of the Chartist movement, and pure trade unionism came once more to dominate the field for years in the English labour movement.

In France also the alliance of Socialism with the labour movement quickly led to attempts on the part of the workers to overthrow the capitalist economic order and pave the way for a new social development. The antagonism between the working class and the bourgeoisie that had just acquired mastery had already shown itself clearly during the storms of the Great Revolution. Before the Revolution the workers had been united in the so-called *Compagnonnages*, whose origin can be traced back to the fifteenth century. These were associations of journeymen craftsmen which had their peculiar ceremonials transmitted from the Middle Ages, whose members were pledged to mutual assistance, and which busied themselves with the concerns of their calling, but also resorted often to strikes and boycotts to protect their immediate economic interests. With the abolition of the guilds and the development of modern industry these bodies gradually lost their importance and gave way to new forms of proletarian organization.

By the law of August 21, 1790, all citizens were conceded the right of free combination within the framework of the existing laws, and the workers availed themselves of this right by organizing themselves in trade unions for the safeguarding of their interests against the employers. A lot of local strike movements ensued, especially in the building industry, and caused the employers a great deal of worry, as the organizations of workers grew constantly stronger, counting 80,000 members in Paris alone.

In a memorial to the government the employers denounced these combinations of workers and demanded the protection of the state against this " new tyranny " which presumed to interfere with the right of free contract between employer and employee. The government responded graciously to this demand and forbade all combinations for the purpose of effecting alterations in the existing conditions of labour, assigning as a reason that it could not permit the existence of a state within the state. This prohibition continued in force until 1864. But here also it was early shown that circumstances are stronger than the law. Just as had the English, so also the French workers resorted to secret associations, since the law denied them the right to urge their demands openly.

The so-called *mutualités*, harmless mutual benefit societies, often served in this connection as a cover, spreading the mantle of legality over the secret organizations for resistance (*sociétés de resistance*). These had, it is true, often to endure harsh persecution and to make many sacrifices, but no law was able to crush their resistance. Under the rule of Louis Philippe the laws against the combination of workers were strengthened still further, but even that could not prevent the steady growth of the *sociétés de resistance*, nor the development of a long series of great strike movements as a result of their underground activities. Of these the fight of the weavers in Lyons in 1831 grew into an event of European importance. Bitter need had spurred these workers to a desperate resistance to the rapacity of the employers, and owing to the interference of the militia this had developed into an outright revolt, into which the workers carried their banner inscribed with the significant words : " Live working or die fighting ! "

As early as the 30's a lot of these workers' associations had become acquainted with Socialist ideas, and after the February Revolution of 1848 this acquaintance afforded the basis for the movement of the French *Workingmen's*

Associations, a co-operative movement with a trade union trend, which worked for a reshaping of society by constructive effort. In his history of the movement S. Engländer puts the number of these associations at about two thousand. But the *coup d'état* of Louis Bonaparte put an abrupt end to this hopeful beginning, as to so many others.

Only with the founding of the *International Workingmen's Association* was there a revival of the doctrines of a militant and constructive Socialism, but after that they spread internationally. The International, which exercised such a powerful influence on the intellectual development of the body of European workers, and which even to-day has not lost its magnetic attraction in the Latin countries, was brought into being by the collaboration of the English and French workers in 1864. It was the first great attempt to unite the workers of all countries in an international alliance which should open the path for the social and economic liberation of the working class. It was from the beginning distinguished from all the political forms of organization of bourgeois radicalism by pointing out that the economic subservience of the workers to the owners of the raw materials and the tools of production was the source of the slavery which revealed itself in social misery, intellectual degradation, and political oppression. For this reason it proclaimed in its statutes the economic liberation of the working class as the great purpose to which every political movement must be subordinate.

Since the most important object was to unite the different factions of the social movement in Europe for this purpose, the organizational structure of the vast workers' alliance was based on the principles of Federalism, which guaranteed to each particular school the possibility of working for this common goal in accordance with their own convictions and on the basis of the peculiar conditions in each country. The International did not stand for any defined social system ; it was rather the expression of a movement whose theoretical principles slowly matured in the practical struggles of everyday life and took clearer form at every stage of its vigorous growth. The first need was to bring the workers of the different countries closer to one another, to make them understand that their economic and social enslavement was everywhere traceable to the same causes, and that consequently the manifestation of their solidarity must reach beyond the artificial boundaries of the states, since it is not tied up with the alleged interests of the nation, but with the lot of their class.

The practical efforts of its sections to end the importation of foreign strike-breakers in times of industrial warfare, and to furnish material and moral assistance to militant workers in every country by international collections, contributed more to the development of an international consciousness among the workers than the loveliest theories could have done. They gave the workers a practical education in social philosophy. It was a fact that after every considerable strike the membership of the International soared mightily, and the conviction of its natural coherence and homogeneity was constantly strengthened.

Thus the International became the great school mistress of the Socialist labour movement and confronted the capitalist world with the world of international labour, which was being ever more firmly welded together in the bonds of proletarian solidarity. The first two congresses of the International, at Geneva in 1866, and at Lausanne in 1867, were characterized by a spirit of comparative moderation. They were the first tentative efforts of a

movement which was only slowly becoming clear as to
its task, and was seeking for a definite expression. But the
great strike movements in France, Belgium, Switzerland,
and other countries gave the International a powerful
forward impetus and revolutionized the minds of the
workers, a change to which the powerful revival during
that period of the democratic ideas, which had suffered
a severe setback after the collapse of the revolutions of
1848-49, contributed not a little.

The congress at Brussels, in 1868, was animated by a
totally different spirit from that of its two predecessors.
It was felt that the workers everywhere were awakening
to new life and were becoming constantly surer of the
object of their endeavours. The congress, by a large
majority, declared itself for the collectivizing of the land
and other means of production, and called upon the
sections in the different countries to go exhaustively into
this question, so that at the next congress a clear decision
could be reached. With this the International took on an
outspokenly Socialistic character, which was most happily
complemented by the outstandingly libertarian tendency
of the workers in the Latin countries. The resolution
to prepare the workers for a general strike to meet the
danger of a threatened war, because they were the only
class that could by energetic intervention prevent the
organized mass murder, also testified to the spirit by
which the International was permeated at that time.

At the congress in Basel, in 1869, the ideational development of the great workers' alliance reached its zenith.
The congress concerned itself only with questions which
had an immediate connection with the economic and
social problems of the working class. It ratified the
resolutions which the Brussels congress had adopted
concerning the collective ownership of the means of

production, leaving the question of the organization of labour open. But the interesting debates at the Basel congress show very plainly that the advanced sections of the International had already been giving attention to this question, and had, moreover, come to very clear conclusions about it. This was revealed particularly in the utterances concerning the importance of trade union organizations to the working class. In the report upon this question which Eugène Hins laid before the congress in the name of the Belgian Federation there was presented for the first time a wholly new point of view, which had an unmistakable resemblance to certain ideas of Owen and the English labour movement of the 30's.

In order to make a correct estimate of this one must remember that the various schools of state-socialism of that time attributed to the trade unions either no importance at all or at best only a subordinate one. The French Blanquists saw in the trade unions merely a reform movement, with which they wished to have nothing to do, as their immediate aim was a Socialist dictatorship. Ferdinand Lassalle directed all his activities toward welding the workers into a political party and was an outspoken opponent of all trade union endeavours, in which he saw only a hindrance to the political evolution of the working class. Marx, and more especially his friends of that period in Germany, recognized, it is true, the necessity of the trade unions for the achievement of certain betterments within the capitalist social system, but they believed that their rôle would be exhausted with this, and that they would disappear along with capitalism, since the transition to Socialism could be guided only by a proletarian dictatorship.

At Basel this idea underwent for the first time a thorough critical examination. In the Belgian report which Hins

laid before the congress, the views expressed in which
were shared by the delegates from Spain, the Swiss Jura,
and a considerable part of the French sections, it was
clearly set forth that the trade union organizations of the
workers not only had a right to existence within the present
society, but they were even more to be regarded as the
social cells of a coming Socialist order, and it was, therefore, the task of the International to educate them for
this service. In accordance with this the congress
adopted the following resolution :

> " The Congress declares that all workers should
> strive to establish associations for resistance in their
> various trades.   As soon as a trade union is formed the
> unions in the same trade are to be notified so that the
> formation of national alliances in the industries may be
> begun.   These alliances shall be charged with the
> duty of collecting all material relating to their industry,
> of advising about measures to be executed in common,
> and of seeing that they are carried out, to the end,
> that the present wage system may be replaced by the
> federation of free producers.   The Congress directs
> the General Council to provide for the alliance of the
> trade unions of all countries."

In his argument for the resolution proposed by the
committee Hins explained that " by this double form of
organization of local workers' associations and general
alliances for each industry on the one hand the political
administration of the committees, and on the other, the
general representation of labour, regional, national and
international, will be provided for. *The councils of the
trade and industrial organizations will take the place of the
present government, and this representation of labour will do
away, once and forever, with the governments of the
past.*"

This new and fruitful idea grew out of the recognition that every new economic form must be accompanied by a new political form of the social organism and could only attain practical expression in this. Therefore, Socialism also had to have a special political form of expression, within which it may become a living thing, and they thought they had found this form in *a system of labour councils*. The workers in the Latin countries, in which the International found its principal support, developed their movement on the basis of economic fighting organizations and Socialist propaganda groups, and worked in the spirit of the Basel resolutions.

As they recognized in the state the political agent and defender of the possessing classes, they did not strive at all for the conquest of political power, but for the overthrow of the state and of every form of political power, in which with sure instinct they saw the requisite preliminary condition for all tyranny and all exploitation. They did, therefore, not choose to imitate the bourgeois classes and set up a political party, thus preparing the way for a new class of professional politicians, whose goal was the conquest of the governing power. They understood that, along with the monopoly of property, the monopoly of power must also be destroyed, if complete reshaping of social life was to be achieved. Proceeding from their recognition that the lordship of man over man had had its day, they sought to familiarize themselves with the administration of things. So to the state politics of the parties they opposed the economic policy of the workers. They understood that the reorganization of society on a Socialist pattern must be carried out in the various branches of industry and in the departments of agrarian production ; of this understanding was born the idea of a system of labour councils.

It was this same idea which inspired large sections of
the Russian workers and peasants at the outbreak of the
revolution, even if the idea had never been thought out
so clearly and systematically in Russia as in the sections
of the First International. Under tsarism the Russian
workers lacked the requisite intellectual preparation for
this. But bolshevism put an abrupt end to this fruitful
idea. For the despotism of dictatorship stands in
irreconcilable contradiction to the constructive idea of
the council system, that is, to a Socialist reconstruction of
society by the producers themselves. The attempt to
combine the two by force could only lead to that soulless
bureaucracy which has been so disastrous for the Russian
Revolution. The council system brooks no dictatorship,
as it proceeds from totally different assumptions. In it
is embodied the will from below, the creative energy of
the toiling masses. In dictatorship, however, lives only
barren compulsion from above, which will suffer no
creative activity and proclaims blind submission as the
highest law for all. The two cannot exist together.
In Russia dictatorship proved victorious. Hence there
are no more soviets there. All that is left of them is
the name and a gruesome caricature of its original
meaning.

The council system for labour embraces a large part
of the economic forms employed by a constructive
Socialism which of its own accord operates and produces
to meet all natural requirements. It was the direct
result of a fruitful development of ideas growing out of
the Socialist labour movement. This particular idea
rose from the effort to provide a concrete basis for the
realization of Socialism. This basis was seen to lie in
the constructive employment of every efficient human
being. But dictatorship is an inheritance from bour-

geois society, the traditional precipitate of French Jacobinism, which was dragged into the proletarian movement by the so-called Babouvists and later taken over by Marx and his followers. The idea of the council system is intimately intergrown with Socialism and is unthinkable without it ; dictatorship, however, has nothing whatever in common with Socialism, and at best can only lead to the most barren of state capitalism.

Dictatorship is a definite form of state power ; the state in state of siege. Like all other advocates of the state idea, so also the advocates of dictatorship proceed from the assumption that any alleged advance and every temporal necessity must be forced upon the people from above. This assumption alone makes dictatorship the greatest obstacle to any social revolution, the proper element of which is the free initiative and constructive activity of the people. Dictatorship is the negation of organic development, of natural building from below upwards, it is the proclamation of the wardship of the toiling people, a guardianship forced upon the masses by a tiny minority. *Even if its supporters are animated by the very best intentions*, the iron logic of the facts will always drive them into the camp of extremest despotism. Russia has given us the most instructive example of this. And the pretence that the so-called *dictatorship of the proletariat* is something different, because we have here to do with the dictatorship of a class, not the dictatorship of individuals, deceives no earnest critic ; it is only a sophisticated trick to fool simpletons. Such a thing as the dictatorship of a class is utterly unthinkable, since there will always be involved merely the dictatorship of a particular party which takes it upon itself to speak *in the name of a class*, just as the bourgeoisie justified any despotic proceeding *in the name of the people*.

The idea of a council system for labour was the practical
overthrow of the state idea as a whole ; it stands, therefore,
in frank antagonism to any form of dictatorship, which
must always have in view the highest development of the
power of the state. The pioneers of this idea in the
First International recognized that economic equality
without political and social liberty is unthinkable ;   for
this reason they were firmly convinced that the liquidation
of all institutions of political power must be the first
task of the social revolution, so as to make any new form
of exploitation impossible. They believed that the
workers' International was destined gradually to gather
all effective workers into its ranks, and at the proper time
to overthrow the economic despotism of the possessing
classes, and along with this all the political coercive
institutions of the capitalist state, and to replace these by
a new order of things. This conviction was held by
all libertarian sections of the International. Bakunin
expressed it in the following words :

" Since the organization of the International has as
its goal, not the setting up of new states or despots,
but the radical destruction of every separate sovereignty,
it must have an essentially different character from the
organization of the state. To just the degree that the
latter is authoritarian, artificial, and violent, alien and
hostile to the natural development of the interests and
the instincts of the people, to that same degree must
the organization of the International be free, natural,
and in every respect in accord with those interests and
instincts. But what is the natural organization of the
masses ? It is one based on the different occupations
of their actual daily life, on their various kinds of work,
organization according to their occupations, trade
organizations. When all industries, including the
various branches of agriculture, are represented in the

International, its organization, the organization of the masses of the people, will be finished."

From this line of thought arose likewise the idea of opposing to the bourgeois parliaments a *Chamber of Labour*, which proceeded from the ranks of the Belgian Internationalists. These labour chambers were to represent the organized labour of every trade and industry, and were to concern themselves with all questions of social economy and economic organization on a Socialist basis, in order to prepare practically for the taking over by the organized workers of the means of production, and in this spirit to provide for the intellectual training of the producers. In addition these bodies were to pass judgment from the workers' point of view on all questions brought up in the bourgeois parliaments which were of interest to the workers, so as to contrast the policies of bourgeois society with the views of the workers. Max Nettlau has given to the public in his book, *Der Anarchismus von Proudhon zu Kropotkin*, a hitherto unknown passage from one of Bakunin's manuscripts that is highly indicative of Bakunin's views on this question :

". . . All this practical and vital study of social science by the workers themselves in their trade sections and in these chambers will, and already has, engendered in them the unanimous, well-considered, theoretically and practically demonstrable conviction that the *serious, final, complete liberation of the workers is possible only upon one condition, that of the appropriation of capital, that is, of raw material and all the tools of labour, including land, by the whole body of workers.* . . . The organization of the trade sections, their federation in the International, and their representation by the Chambers of Labour, not only create a great academy, in which the workers of the International,

combining theory and practice, can and must study
economic science, they also bear in themselves the
living germs of *the new social order*, which is to replace
the bourgeois world. They are creating not only the
ideas but also the facts of the future itself. . . ."

These ideas were at that time generally disseminated
in the sections of the International in Belgium, Holland,
the Swiss Jura, France and Spain, and gave to the
Socialism of the great workers' alliance a peculiar
character, which with the development of political labour
parties in Europe was for a considerable time almost
completely forgotten, and only in Spain never exhausted
its power to win converts, as recent events in that country
have so clearly shown.   They found active advocates in
men like James Guillaume, Adhémar Schwitzguébel,
Eugène Varlin, Louis Pindy, César De Paepe, Eugène
Hins, Hector Denis, Guillaume De Greef, Victor Arnould,
R. Farga Pellicer, G. Sentiñon, Anselmo Lorenzo, to
mention here only the best-known names, all men of
excellent reputation in the International.   The fact is
that the whole intellectual development of the International is to be ascribed to the enthusiasm of these
libertarian elements in it, and received no stimulus from
either the state Socialist factions in Germany and
Switzerland or pure Trades Unionism in England.

So long as the International pursued these general
lines, and for the rest respected the right of decision of
the separate federations, as was provided in its statutes,
it exercised an irresistible influence over the organized
workers.   But that changed at once when Marx and
Engels began to use their position in the London General
Council to commit the separate national federations to
parliamentary action.   This occurred first at the unhappy London Conference of 1871.   This behaviour

was in sharp violation not only of the spirit but also of
the statutes of the International. It could but encounter
the united resistance of all the libertarian elements in
the International, the more so as the question had never
previously been brought before a congress for consideration.

Shortly after the London Conference the Jura Federation published the historic circular of Sonvillier, which
protested in determined and unequivocal words against
the arrogant presumption of the London General Council.
But the congress at The Hague in 1872, in which a
majority had been artificially created by the employment
of the dirtiest and most reprehensible methods, crowned
the work begun by the London Conference of trans-
forming the International into an electoral machine.
In order to obviate any misunderstanding the Blanquist,
Edouard Vaillant, in his argument for the resolution
proposed by the General Council advocating the conquest
of political power by the working class, explained that
" as soon as this resolution has been adopted by the
Congress and so incorporated in the Bible of the International, it will be the duty of every member to follow
it under penalty of expulsion." By this Marx and his
followers directly provoked the open split in the International with all its disastrous consequences for the
development of the labour movement, and inaugurated
the period of parliamentary politics which of natural
necessity led to that intellectual stagnation and moral
degeneration in the Socialist movement which we can
observe to-day in most countries.

Soon after the Hague Congress the delegates of the
most important and energetic federations of the International met in the anti-authoritarian congress in St.
Immier, which declared all the resolutions adopted at

The Hague null and void. From then on dates the split
in the Socialist camp between the advocates of direct
revolutionary action and the spokesmen for parliamentary
politics, which with the lapse of time has grown constantly wider and more unbridgable.   Marx and Bakunin
were merely the most prominent representatives of the
opposed factions in this struggle between two different
conceptions of the fundamental principles of Socialism.
But it would be a big mistake to try to explain this struggle
as merely a conflict between two personalities ; it was
the antagonism between two sets of ideas which gave to
this struggle its real importance, and still gives it to-day.
That Marx and Engels gave such a spiteful and personal
character to the dissension was a disaster.   The International had room for every faction, and a continuous
discussion of the different views could only have
contributed to their clarification.   But the effort to make
all schools of thought subservient to one particular school,
one which, moreover, represented only a small minority
in the International, could but lead to a cleavage and to
the decline of the great alliance of workers, could but
destroy those promising germs which were of such great
importance to the labour movement in every land.

The Franco-Prussian War, by which the focal point
of the Socialist movement was transferred to Germany,
whose workers had neither revolutionary traditions nor
that rich experience possessed by Socialists in the
countries to the west, contributed greatly to this decline.
The defeat of the Paris Commune and the incipient
reaction in France, which in a few years spread over Spain
and Italy as well, pushed the fruitful idea of a council
system for labour far into the background.   The sections
of the International in those countries were for a long
time able to carry on only an underground existence and

were obliged to concentrate all their strength on repelling the reaction. Only with the awakening of revolutionary Syndicalism in France were the creative ideas of the First International rescued from oblivion, once more to vitalize the Socialist labour movement.

4

THE OBJECTIVES OF ANARCHO-SYNDICALISM

Anarcho-Syndicalism versus political Socialism ; Political parties and labour unions ; Federalism versus Centralism ; Germany and Spain ; The organization of Anarcho-Syndicalism ; The impotence of political parties for social reconstruction ; The C.N.T. in Spain : its aims and methods ; Constructive work of the labour syndicates and peasant collectives in Spain ; Anarcho-Syndicalism and national politics ; Problems of our time.

MODERN Anarcho-Syndicalism is a direct continuation of those social aspirations which took shape in the bosom of the First International and which were best understood and most strongly held by the libertarian wing of the great workers' alliance. Its present day representatives are the federations in the different countries of the revived *International Workingmen's Association* of 1922, the most important of which is the powerful Federation of Labour (*Confederación National del Trabajo*) in Spain. Its theoretical assumptions are based on the teachings of Libertarian or Anarchist Socialism, while its form of organization is largely borrowed from revolutionary Syndicalism, which in the years from 1900 to 1910 experienced a marked upswing, particularly in France. It stands in direct opposition to the political Socialism of our day, represented by the parliamentary labour parties in the different countries. While in the time of the First International barely the first beginnings of these parties existed in Germany, France, and Switzerland, to-day we are in a position to estimate the results of their tactics for Socialism and the labour movement after more than sixty years' activity in all countries.

Participation in the politics of the bourgeois states has not brought the labour movement a hair's-breadth nearer to Socialism, but, thanks to this method, Socialism has almost been completely crushed and condemned to insignificance. The ancient proverb : " Who eats of the pope, dies of him," has held true in this content also ; who eats of the state is ruined by it. Participation in parliamentary politics has affected the Socialist labour movement like an insidious poison. It destroyed the belief in the necessity of constructive Socialist activity and, worst of all, the impulse to self-help, by inoculating people with the ruinous delusion that salvation always comes from above.

Thus, in place of the creative Socialism of the old International, there developed a sort of substitute product which has nothing in common with real Socialism but the name. Socialism steadily lost its character of a cultural ideal, which was to prepare the peoples for the dissolution of capitalist society, and, therefore, could not let itself be halted by the artificial frontiers of the national states. In the minds of the leaders of this new phase of the Socialist movement the interests of the national state were blended more and more with the alleged aims of their party, until at last they became unable to distinguish any definite boundaries whatever between them. So inevitably the labour movement was gradually incorporated in the equipment of the national state and restored to this the equilibrium which it had actually lost before.

It would be a mistake to find in this strange about-face
an intentional betrayal by the leaders, as has so often
been done. The truth is that we have to do here with a
gradual assimilation to the modes of thought of capitalist
society, which is a condition of the practical activity of
the labour parties of to-day, and which necessarily
affects the intellectual attitude of their political leaders.
Those very parties which had once set out to conquer
political power under the flag of Socialism saw themselves
compelled by the iron logic of conditions to sacrifice their
Socialist convictions bit by bit to the national policies
of the state. They became, without the majority of their
adherents ever becoming aware of it, political lightning
rods for the security of the capitalist social order. The
political power which they had wanted to conquer had
gradually conquered their Socialism until there was
scarcely anything left of it.

Parliamentarism, which quickly attained a dominating
position in the labour parties of the different countries,
lured a lot of bourgeois minds and career-hungry
politicians into the Socialist camp, and this helped to
accelerate the internal decay of original Socialist principles.
Thus Socialism in course of time lost its creative initiative
and became an ordinary reform movement which lacked
any element of greatness. People were content with
successes at the polls, and no longer attributed any
importance whatever to social upbuilding and constructive
education of the workers for this end. The consequences
of this disastrous neglect of one of the weightiest problems,
one of decisive importance for the realization of Socialism,
were revealed in their full scope when, after the World
War, a revolutionary situation arose in many of the
countries of Europe. The collapse of the old system
had, in several states, put into the hands of the Socialists

the power they had striven for so long and pointed to as
the first pre-requisite for the realization of Socialism.
In Russia the seizure of power by the left wing of state
Socialism in the form of Bolshevism paved the way, not
for a Socialist society, but for the most primitive type
of bureaucratic state capitalism and a reversion to the
political absolutism which was long ago abolished in
most countries by bourgeois revolutions. In Germany,
however, where the moderate wing in the form of Social
Democracy attained to power, Socialism, in its long years
of absorption in routine parliamentary tasks, had become
so bogged down that it was no longer capable of any
creative act whatever. Even a bourgeois democratic
sheet like the *Frankfurter Zeitung* felt obliged to confirm
that " the history of European peoples has not previously
produced a revolution that has been so poor in creative
ideas and so weak in revolutionary energy."

But that was not all : not only was political Socialism
in no position to undertake any kind of constructive
effort in the direction of Socialism, it did not even possess
the moral strength to hold on to the achievements of
bourgeois Democracy and Liberalism, and surrendered
the country without resistance to Fascism, which smashed
the entire labour movement to bits with one blow. It
had become so deeply immersed in the bourgeois state
that it had lost all sense of constructive Socialist action
and felt itself tied to the barren routine of everyday
practical politics as a galley-slave was chained to his
bench.

Modern Anarcho-Syndicalism is the direct reaction
against the concepts and methods of political Socialism,
a reaction which even before the war had already made
itself manifest in the strong upsurge of the Syndicalist
labour movement in France, Italy, and other countries,

not to speak of Spain, where the great majority of the organized workers had always remained faithful to the doctrines of the First International.

The term " workers' syndicate " meant in France at first merely a trade union organization of producers for the immediate betterment of their economic and social status. But the rise of revolutionary Syndicalism gave this original meaning a much wider and deeper import. Just as the party is, so to speak, the unified organization for definite political effort within the modern constitutional state, and seeks to maintain the bourgeois order in one form or another, so, according to the Syndicalist view, the trade union, the syndicate, is the unified organization of labour and has for its purpose the defence of the interests of the producers within existing society and the preparing for and the practical carrying out of the reconstruction of social life after the pattern of Socialism. It has, therefore, a double purpose : 1. As the fighting organization of the workers against the employers to enforce the demands of the workers for the safeguarding and raising of their standard of living ; 2. As the school for the intellectual training of the workers to make them acquainted with the technical management of production and economic life in general, so that when a revolutionary situation arises they will be capable of taking the socio-economic organism into their own hands and remaking it according to Socialist principles.

Anarcho-Syndicalists are of the opinion that political parties, even when they bear a Socialist name, are not fitted to perform either of these two tasks. The mere fact that, even in those countries where political Socialism commanded powerful organizations and had millions of voters behind it, the workers had never been able to dispense with trade unions, because legislation offered them no protection in their struggle for daily bread, testifies to this. It frequently happened that in just those sections of the country where the Socialist parties were strongest the wages of workers were lowest and the conditions of labour worst. That was the case, for example, in the northern industrial districts of France, where Socialists were in the majority in numerous city administrations, and in Saxony and Silesia, where throughout its existence German Social Democracy had been able to show a large following.

Governments and Parliaments seldom decide on economic or social reforms on their own initiative, and where this has happened thus far the alleged improvements have always remained a dead letter in the vast waste of laws. Thus the modest attempts of the English parliament in the early period of big industry, when the legislators, frightened by the horrible effects of the exploitation of children, at last resolved on some trifling ameliorations, for a long time had almost no effect. On the one hand they ran afoul of the lack of understanding of the workers themselves, on the other they were sabotaged outright by the employers. It was much the same with the well-known law which the Italian government enacted in the middle 90's to forbid women who were compelled to toil in the sulphur mines in Sicily from taking their children down into the pits with them. This law also remained a dead letter, because these unfortunate women were so poorly paid that they were obliged to disregard the law. Only a considerable time later, when these working women had succeeded in organizing, and thus forcing up their standard of living, did the evil disappear of itself. There are plenty of similar instances in the history of every country.

But even the legal authorization of a reform is no

guarantee of its permanence unless there exist outside of
parliament militant masses who are ready to defend it
against every attack.   Thus the English factory owners,
despite enactment of the ten-hour law in 1848, shortly
afterward availed themselves of an industrial crisis to
compel workers to toil for eleven or even twelve hours.
When the factory inspectors took legal proceedings
against individual employers on this account, the accused
were not only acquitted, the government hinted to the
inspectors that they were not to insist on the letter of the
law, so that the workers were obliged, after economic
conditions had revived somewhat, to make the fight for
the ten-hour day all over again on their own resources.
Among the few economic improvements which the
November Revolution of 1918 brought to the German
workers, the eight-hour day was the most important.
But it was snatched back from the workers by the employers in most industries, despite the fact that it was in
the statutes, actually anchored legally in the Weimar
Constitution itself.

But if political parties are absolutely incapable of
making the slightest contribution to the improvement of
the standard of living of the workers within present day
society, they are far less able to carry on the organic
upbuilding of a Socialist community or even to pave the
way for it, since they utterly lack every practical require-
ment for such an achievement.   Russia and Germany
have given quite sufficient proof of this.

The lancehead of the labour movement is, therefore,
not the political party but the trade union, toughened by
daily combat and permeated by Socialist spirit.   Only
in the realm of economy are the workers able to display
their full social strength, for it is their activity as producers
which holds together the whole social structure, and

guarantees the existence of society at all. In any other field they are fighting on alien soil and wasting their strength in hopeless struggles which bring them not an iota nearer to the goal of their desires. In the field of parliamentary politics the worker is like the giant Antæus of the Greek legend, whom Hercules was able to strangle in the air after he had lifted his feet off the earth who was his mother. Only as producer and creator of social wealth does he become aware of his strength ; in solidaric union with his fellows he creates in the trade union the invincible phalanx which can withstand any assault, if it is aflame with the spirit of freedom and animated by the ideal of social justice.

For the Anarcho-Syndicalists the trade union is by no means a mere transitory phenomenon bound up with the duration of capitalist society, it is the germ of the Socialist economy of the future, the elementary school of Socialism in general. Every new social structure makes organs for itself in the body of the old organism. Without this preliminary any social evolution is unthinkable. Even revolutions can only develop and mature the germs which already exist and have made their way into the consciousness of men ; they cannot themselves create these germs or generate new worlds out of nothing. It therefore concerns us to plant these germs while there is yet time and bring them to the strongest possible development, so as to make the task of the coming social revolution easier and to insure its permanence.

All the educational work of the Anarcho-Syndicalists is aimed at this purpose. Education for Socialism does not mean for them trivial campaign propaganda and so-called " politics of the day," but the effort to make clear to the workers the intrinsic connections among social problems, by technical instruction and the development of their administrative capacities, to prepare them for their rôle of re-shapers of economic life, and give them the moral assurance required for the performance of their task. No social body is better fitted for this purpose than the economic fighting organization of the workers ; it gives a definite direction to their social activities and toughens their resistance in the immediate struggle for the necessities of life and the defence of their human rights. This direct and unceasing warfare with the supporters of the present system develops at the same time the ethical concepts without which any social transformation is impossible : vital solidarity with their fellows-in-destiny and moral responsibility for their own actions.

Just because the educational work of the Anarcho-Syndicalists is directed toward the development of independent thought and action, they are outspoken opponents of all those centralizing tendencies which are so characteristic of political labour parties. But centralism, that artificial organization from above downward which turns over the affairs of everybody in a lump to a small minority, is always attended by barren official routine ; and this crushes individual conviction, kills all personal initiative by lifeless discipline and bureaucratic ossification, and permits no independent action. The organization of Anarcho-Syndicalism is based on the principles of Federalism, on free combination from below upward, putting the right of self-determination of every member above everything else and recognizing only the organic agreement of all on the basis of like interests and common convictions.

It has often been charged against Federalism that it divides the forces and cripples the strength of organized resistance, and, very significantly, it has been just the representatives of the political labour parties and of the trade unions under their influence who have kept repeating this charge to the point of nausea. But here, too, the facts of life have spoken more clearly than any theory. There was no country in the world where the whole labour movement was so completely centralized and the technique of organization developed to such extreme perfection as in Germany before Hitler's accession to power. A powerful bureaucratic apparatus covered the whole country and determined every political and economic expression of the organized workers. In the very last elections the Social Democratic and Communist parties united over twelve million voters for their candidates. But after Hitler seized power six million organized workers did not raise a finger to avert the catastrophe which had plunged Germany into the abyss, and which in a few months beat their organizations completely to pieces.

But in Spain, where Anarcho-Syndicalism had maintained its hold upon organized labour from the days of the First International, and by untiring libertarian propaganda and sharp fighting had trained it to resistance, it was the powerful C.N.T. which by the boldness of its action frustrated the criminal plans of Franco and his numerous helpers at home and abroad, and by their heroic example spurred the Spanish workers and peasants to the battle against Fascism—a fact which Franco himself has been compelled to acknowledge. Without the heroic resistance of the Anarcho-Syndicalist labour unions the Fascist reaction would in a few weeks have dominated the whole country.

When one compares the technique of the federalist organization of the C.N.T. with the centralistic machine which the German workers had built for themselves, one is surprised at the simplicity of the former. In the smaller syndicates every task for the organization was performed voluntarily. In the larger alliances, where naturally established official representatives were necessary, these were elected for one year only and received the same pay as the workers in their trade. Even the General Secretary of the C.N.T. was no exception to this rule. This is an old tradition which has been kept up in Spain since the days of the International. This simple form of organization not only sufficed the Spanish workers for turning the C.N.T. into a fighting unit of the first rank, it also safeguarded them against any bureaucratic regime in their own ranks and helped them to display that irresistible spirit of solidarity and tenacious belligerence which is so characteristic of this organization, and which one encounters in no other country.

For the state centralism is the appropriate form of organization, since it aims at the greatest possible uniformity in social life for the maintenance of political and social equilibrium. But for a movement whose very existence depends on prompt action at any favourable moment and on the independent thought and action of its supporters, centralism could but be a curse, by weakening its power of decision and systematically repressing all immediate action. If, for example, as was the case in Germany, every local strike had first to be approved by the Central, which was often hundreds of miles away and was usually not in a position to pass a correct judgment on the local conditions, one cannot wonder that the inertia of the apparatus of organization renders a quick attack quite impossible, and there thus arises a state of affairs where the energetic and intellectually alert groups no longer serve as patterns for the less active, but are condemned by these to inactivity, inevitably bringing the whole movement to stagnation. Organization is, after all, only a means to an end. When it becomes an end in itself, it kills the spirit and the vital initiative of its members and sets up that domination by mediocrity which is the characteristic of all bureaucracies.

Anarcho-Syndicalists are, therefore, of the opinion that trade union organization should be of such a character as to afford workers the possibility of achieving the utmost in their struggle against the employers, and at the same time provide them with a basis from which they will be able in a revolutionary situation to proceed with the reshaping of economic and social life.

Their organization is accordingly constructed on the following principles : The workers in each locality join the unions of their respective trades, and these are subject to the veto of no Central but enjoy the entire right of self-determination. The trade unions of a city or a rural district combine in a so-called labour cartel. The labour cartels constitute the centres for local propaganda and education ; they weld the workers together as a class and prevent the rise of any narrow-minded factional spirit. In times of local labour trouble they arrange for the solidaric co-operation of the whole body of organized labour in the use of every agency available under the circumstances. All the labour cartels are grouped according to districts and regions to form the National Federation of Labour Cartels, which maintain the permanent connection between the local bodies, arranges for free adjustment of the productive labour of the members of the different organizations on co-operative lines, provide for the necessary co-ordination in the work of education, in which the stronger cartels will need to

come to aid of the weaker ones, and in general support
the local groups with council and guidance.

Every trade union is, moreover, federatively allied with
all the organizations in the same trade throughout the
country, and these in turn with all related trades, so that
all are combined in general industrial alliances. It is
the task of these alliances to arrange for the co-operative
action of the local groups, to conduct solidaric strikes
where the necessity arises, and to meet all the demands of
the day-to-day struggle between capital and labour.
Thus the Federation of Labour Cartels and the Federation
of Industrial Alliances constitute the two poles about
which the whole life of the trade unions revolves.

Such a form of organization not only gives the workers
every opportunity for direct action in their struggles for
daily bread, it also provides them with the necessary
preliminaries for carrying through the reorganization of
social life on a Socialist plan by their own strength and
without alien intervention, in case of a revolutionary
crisis.   Anarcho-Syndicalists are convinced that a
Socialist economic order cannot be created by the decrees
and statutes of a government, but only by the solidaric
collaboration of the workers with hand or brain in each
special branch of production ; that is, through the taking
over of the management of all plants by the producers
themselves under such form that the separate groups,
plants, and branches of industry are independent members
of the general economic organism and systematically carry
on production and the distribution of the products in
the interest of the community on the basis of free mutual
agreements.

In such a case the labour cartels would take over the
existing social capital in each community, determine the
needs of the inhabitants of their districts, and organize

local consumption. Through the agency of the national Federation of Labour Cartels it would be possible to calculate the total requirements of the country and adjust the work of production accordingly. On the other hand, it would be the task of the Industrial Alliances to take control of all the instruments of production, machines, raw materials, means of transportation, and the like, and to provide the separate producing groups with what they need. In a word : 1. Organization of the plants by the producers themselves and direction of the work by labour councils elected by them. 2. Organization of the total production of the country by the industrial and agricultural alliances. 3. Organization of consumption by the Labour Cartels.

In this respect, also, practical experience has given the best instruction. It has shown us that economic questions in the Socialist meaning cannot be solved by a government, even when by that is meant the celebrated *dictatorship of the proletariat.* In Russia the Bolshevist dictatorship stood for almost two whole years helpless before its economic problems and tried to hide its incapacity behind a flood of decrees and ordinances, of which ninety-nine per cent. were buried at once in the various bureaus. If the world could be set free by decrees, there would long ago have been no problems left in Russia. In its fanatical zeal for government, Bolshevism has violently destroyed just the most valuable beginnings of a Socialist social order, by suppressing the co-operatives, bringing the trade unions under state control, and depriving the soviets of their independence almost from the beginning. Kropotkin said with justice in his " Message to the Workers of the West-European Countries " :

" Russia has shown us the way in which Socialism cannot be realized, although the populace, nauseated

with the old regime, opposed no active resistance to
the experiments of the new government. The idea
of workers' councils for the control of the political and
economic life of the country is, in itself, of extraordinary importance. . . . But so long as the country
is dominated by the dictatorship of a party, the workers'
and peasants' councils naturally lose their significance.
They are thereby degraded to the same passive rôle
which the representatives of the estates used to play
in the time of the absolute monarchies. A workers'
council ceases to be a free and valuable adviser when
no free press exists in the country, as has been the case
with us for over two years. Worse still : the workers'
and peasants' councils lose all their meaning when no
public propaganda takes place before their election,
and the elections themselves are conducted under the
pressure of party dictatorship. Such a ' government
by councils ' (soviet government) amounts to a definite
step backward as soon as the Revolution advances to
the erection of a new society on a new ecomonic basis :
it becomes just a dead principle on a new foundation."

The course of events has proved Kropotkin right on
every point. Russia is to-day farther from Socialism
than any other country. Dictatorship does not lead to
the economic and social liberation of the toiling masses,
but to the suppression of even the most trivial freedom
and the development of an unlimited despotism which
respects no rights and treads underfoot every feeling of
human dignity. What the Russian worker has gained
economically under this regime is a most ruinous form
of human exploitation, borrowed from the most extreme
stage of capitalism, in the shape of the Stakhanov system,
which raises his productive capacity to its highest limit
and degrades him to a galley slave, who is denied all
control of his personal labour, and who must submit to

every order of his superiors if he does not wish to expose himself to penalties of life and liberty. But compulsory labour is the last road that can lead to Socialism. It estranges the man from the community, destroys his joy in his daily work, and stifles that sense of personal responsibility to his fellows without which there can be no talk of Socialism at all.

We shall not even speak of Germany here. One could not reasonably expect of a party like the Social Democrats —whose central organ, *Vorwärts*, just on the evening before the November Revolution of 1918, warned the workers against precipitancy, " as the German people are not ready for a republic "—that it would experiment with Socialism. Power, we might say, fell into its lap over-night, and it actually did not know what to do with it. Its absolute impotence contributed not a little to enabling Germany to bask to-day in the sun of the *Third Reich*.

The Anarcho-Syndicalist labour unions of Spain, and especially of Catalonia, where their influence is strongest, have shown us an example in this respect which is unique in the history of the Socialist labour movement. In this they only confirmed what the Anarcho-Syndicalists have always insisted on : that the approach to Socialism is possible only when the workers have created the necessary organism for it, and when above all they have previously prepared for it by a genuinely Socialistic education and direct action. But this was the case in Spain, where since the days of the International the weight of the labour movement had lain, not in political parties, but in the revolutionary trade unions.

When, on July 19, 1936, the conspiracy of the Fascist generals ripened into open revolt and was put down in a few days by the heroic resistance of the C.N.T. (National Federation of Labour) and the F.A.I. (Anarchist Federation of Iberia), ridding Catalonia of the enemy and frustrating the plan of the conspirators, based as it was on sudden surprise, it was clear that the Catalonian workers could not stop half way. So there followed the collectivizing of the land and the taking over of the plants by the workers' and peasants' syndicates ; and this movement, which was released by the initiative of the C.N.T. and the F.A.I., with irrestible power overran Aragon, the Levante, and other sections of the country, and even swept along with it a large part of the trade unions of the Socialist Party, organized in the U.G.T. (General Labour Union). The revolt of the Fascists had set Spain on the road to a social revolution.

This same event reveals that the Anarcho-Syndicalist workers of Spain not only know how to fight, but that they are filled with that great constructive spirit derived from their many years of Socialist education. It is the great merit of Libertarian Socialism in Spain, which now finds expression in the C.N.T. and the F.A.I., that since the days of the First International it has trained the workers in that spirit which treasures freedom above all else and regards the intellectual independence of its adherents as the basis of its existence. The libertarian labour movement in Spain has never lost itself in the labyrinth of an economic metaphysics which crippled its intellectual buoyancy by fatalistic conceptions, as was the case in Germany ; nor has it unprofitably wasted its energy in the barren routine tasks of bourgeois parliaments. Socialism was for it a concern of the people, an organic growth proceeding from the activity of the masses themselves and having its basis in their economic organizations.

Therefore the C.N.T. is not simply an alliance of industrial workers like the trade unions in every other country. It embraces within its ranks also the syndicates of the peasants and field-workers as well as those of the brain-workers and the intellectuals. If the Spanish peasants are now fighting shoulder to shoulder with city workers against Fascism, it is the result of the great work of Socialist education which has been performed by the C.N.T. and its forerunners. Socialists of all schools, genuine liberals, and bourgeois anti-Fascists who have had an opportunity to observe on the spot have thus far passed only one judgment on the creative capacity of the C.N.T., and have accorded to its constructive labours the highest admiration. Not one of them could help extolling the natural intelligence, the thoughtfulness and prudence, and above all the unexampled tolerance with which the workers and peasants of the C.N.T. have gone about their difficult task.[1] Workers, peasants,

[1] Here are just a few opinions of foreign journalists who have no personal connection with the Anarchist movement. Thus, Andres Oltmares, professor in the University of Geneva, in the course of an address of some length, said :

"In the midst of the civil war the Anarchists have proved themselves to be political organizers of the first rank. They kindled in everyone the required sense of responsibility, and knew how, by eloquent appeals, to keep alive the spirit of sacrifice for the general welfare of the people.

"As a Social Democrat I speak here with inner joy and sincere admiration of my experiences in Catalonia. The anti-capitalist transformation took place here without their having to resort to a dictatorship. The members of the syndicates are their own masters and carry on production and the distribution of the products of labour under their own management, with the advice of technical experts in whom they have confidence. The enthusiasm of the workers is so great that they scorn any personal advantage and are concerned only for the welfare of all."

The well-known Italian anti-Fascist, Carlo Rosselli, who before Mussolini's accession to power was professor of economics in the University of Genoa, put his judgment into the following words :

"In three months Catalonia has been able to set up a new social order on the ruins of an ancient system. This is chiefly due to the Anarchists, who have revealed a quite remarkable sense of proportion, realistic understanding, and organizing

technicians, and men of science had come together for co-operative work, and in three months gave an entirely new character to the whole economic life of Catalonia.

In Catalonia to-day three-fourths of the land is collectivized and co-operatively cultivated by the peasants' syndicates. In this each community presents a type by itself and adjusts its internal affairs in its own way, but settles economic questions through the agency of its Federation. Thus there is preserved the possibility of free enterprise, inciting new ideas and mutual stimulation. One-fourth of the country is in the hands of small peasant proprietors, to whom has been left the free choice between joining the collectives or continuing their family husbandry. In many instances their small holdings have even been increased in proportion to the size of their families. In Aragon an overwhelming majority of the peasants declared for collective cultivation. There are

ability . . . All the revolutionary forces of Catalonia have united in a programme of Syndicalist-Socialist character : socialization of large industry ; recognition of the small proprietor ; workers' control . . . Anarcho-Syndicalism, hitherto so despised, has revealed itself as a great constructive force . . . I am not an Anarchist, but I regard it as my duty to express here my opinion of the Anarchists of Catalonia, who have all too often been represented to the world as a destructive, if not as a criminal, element. I was with them at the front, in the trenches, and I have learned to admire them. The Catalonian Anarchists belong in the advance guard of the coming revolution. A new world was born with them, and it is a joy to serve that world."

And Fenner Brockway, Secretary of the I.L.P. in England, who travelled in Spain after the May events in Catalonia (1937), expressed his impressions in the following words :

" I was impressed by the strength of the C.N.T. It was unnecessary to tell me that it is the largest and most vital of the working-class organizations in Spain. That was evident on all sides. The large industries were clearly, in the main, in the hands of the C.N.T.—railways, road transport, shipping, engineering, textiles, electricity, building, agriculture. At Valencia the U.G.T. had a greater share of control than in Barcelona, but generally speaking the mass of manual workers belonged to the

in that province over four hundred collective farms, of which about ten are under the control of the Socialist U.G.T., while all the rest are conducted by syndicates of the C.N.T. Agriculture has made such advances there that in the course of a year forty per cent. of the formerly untilled land has been brought under cultivation. In the Levante, in Andalusia and Castile, also, collective agriculture under the management of the syndicates is making constantly greater advances. In numerous smaller communities a Socialist form of life has already become naturalized, the inhabitants no longer carrying on exchange by means of money, but satisfying their needs out of the product of their collective industry and conscientiously devoting the surplus to the support of their comrades fighting at the front.

In most of the rural collectives individual compensation for work performed has been retained, and the further

---

C.N.T. The U.G.T. membership was more of the type of the ' white-collar ' worker . . . I was immensely impressed by the constructive revolutionary work which is being done by the C.N.T. Their achievement of workers' control in industry is an inspiration. One could take the example of the railways or engineering or textiles . . . There are still some Britishers and Americans who regard the Anarchists of Spain as impossible, undisciplined uncontrollables. This is poles away from the truth. The Anarchists of Spain, through the C.N.T., are doing one of the biggest constructive jobs ever done by the working-class. At the front they are fighting Fascism. Behind the front they are actually constructing the new Workers' Society. They see that the war against Fascism and the carrying through of the Social Revolution are inseparable. Those who have seen and understood what they are doing must honour them and be grateful to them. They are resisting Fascism. They are at the same time creating the New Workers' Order which is the only alternative to Fascism. That is surely the biggest thing now being done by the workers in any part of the world." And in another place : " The great solidarity that existed among the Anarchists was due to each individual relying on his own strength and not depending on leadership . . . The organisations must, to be successful, be combined with a free-thinking people ; not a mass, but free individuals."

upbuilding of the new system postponed until the ter-
mination of the war, which at present claims the entire
strength of the people.   In these the amount of the wages
is determined by the size of the families.   The economic
reports in the daily bulletins of the C.N.T. are extremely
interesting, with their accounts of the building-up of the
collectives and their technical development through the
introduction of machines and chemical fertilizers, which
had been almost unknown before.   The agricultural
collectives in Castile alone have during the past year
spent more than two million pesetas for this purpose.
The great task of collectivizing the land was made much
easier after the rural federations of the U.G.T. joined
the general movement.   In many communities all affairs
are arranged jointly by delegates of the C.N.T. and the
U.G.T., bringing about a rapprochement of the two
organizations which culminated in an alliance of the
workers in the two organizations.

But the workers' syndicates have made their most
astounding achievements in the field of industry, since
they took into their hands the administration of industrial
life as a whole.   In Catalonia in the course of a year the
railroads were fitted out with a complete modern equipment, and in punctuality the service reached a point that
had been hitherto unknown.   The same advances were
achieved in the entire transport system, in the textile
industry, in machine construction, in building, and in the
small industries.   But in the war industries the syndicates
have performed a genuine miracle.   By the so-called
neutrality pact the Spanish government was prevented
from importing from abroad any considerable quantities
of war materials.   But Catalonia before the Fascist
revolt had not a single plant for the manufacture of army
equipment.   The first concern was, therefore, to re-make

whole industries to meet the war demands. A hard task for the syndicates, which already had their hands full setting up a new social order. But they performed it with an energy and a technical efficiency that can be explained only by the devotion of the workers and their boundless readiness to make sacrifices for their cause. Men toiled in the factories twelve and fourteen hours a day to bring the great work to completion. To-day Catalonia possesses 283 huge plants which are operating day and night in the production of war materials, so that the fronts may be kept supplied. At present Catalonia is providing for the greater part of all war demands. Professor Andres Oltmares declared in the course of an article that in this field the workers' syndicates of Catalonia " had accomplished in seven weeks as much as France did in fourteen months after the outbreak of the World War."

But that is not all by a great deal. The unhappy war brought into Catalonia an overwhelming flood of fugitives from all the war-swept districts in Spain ; their number has to-day grown to a million. Over fifty per cent. of the sick and wounded in the hospitals of Catalonia are not Catalonians. One understands, therefore, with what a task the workers' syndicates were confronted in the meeting of all these demands. Of the re-organization of the whole educational system by the teachers' groups in the C.N.T., the associations for the protection of works of art, and a hundred other matters we cannot even make mention here.

During this same time the C.N.T. was maintaining 120,000 of its militia, who were fighting on all fronts. No other organization in Spain has thus far made such sacrifices of life and limb as the C.N.T.-F.A.I. In its heroic stand against Fascism it has lost a lot of its most

distinguished fighters, among them Francisco Ascaso and
Buenaventura Durruti, whose epic greatness made him
the hero of the Spanish people.

Under these circumstances it is, perhaps, under-
standable that the syndicates have not thus far been able
to bring to completion their great task of social reconstruction, and for the time being were unable to give
their full attention to the organization of consumption.
The war, the possession by the Fascist armies of important
sources of raw materials, the German and Italian invasion,
the hostile attitude of foreign capital, the onslaughts of
the counter-revolution in the country itself, which,
significantly, was befriended this time by Russia and the
Communist Party of Spain—all this and many other
things have compelled the syndicates to postpone many
great and important tasks until the war is brought to a
victorious conclusion. But by taking the land and the
industrial plants under their own management they have
taken the first and most important step on the road to
Socialism. Above all, they have proved *that the workers,
even without the capitalists, are able to carry on production
and to do it better than a lot of profit-hungry entrepreneurs.*
Whatever the outcome of the bloody war in Spain may
be, to have given this great demonstration remains the
indisputable service of the Spanish Anarcho-Syndicalists,
whose heroic example has opened for the Socialist movement new outlooks for the future.

If the Anarcho-Syndicalists are striving to implant in
the working classes in every country an understanding of
this new form of constructive Socialism, and to show them
that they must, to-day, give to their economic fighting
organizations the forms necessary to enable them during
a general economic crisis to carry through the work of
Socialist upbuilding, this does not mean that these forms

must everywhere be cut to the same pattern. In every country there are special conditions which are intimately intergrown with its historical development, its traditions, and its peculiar psychological assumptions. The great superiority of Federalism is, indeed, just that it takes these important matters into account and does not insist on a uniformity that does violence to free thought, and forces on men from without things contrary to their inner inclination.

Kropotkin once said that, taking England as an example, there existed there three great movements which, at the time of a revolutionary crisis, would enable the workers to carry through a complete overturn of social economy : trades unionism, the co-operative organizations, and the movement for municipal Socialism ; provided that they had a fixed goal in view and worked together according to a definite plan. The workers must learn that, not only must their social liberation be their own work, but that that liberation was possible only if they themselves attended to the constructive preliminaries instead of leaving the task to the politicians, who were in no way fitted for it. And above all they must understand that however different the immediate preliminaries for their liberation might be in different countries, the effects of capitalist exploitation are everywhere the same and they must, therefore, give to their efforts the necessary international character.

Above all they must not tie up these efforts with the interests of the national states, as has, unfortunately, happened in most countries hitherto. The world of organized labour must pursue its own ends, as it has its own interests to defend, and these are not identical with those of the state or those of the possessing classes. A collaboration of workers and employers such as was

advocated by the Socialist Party and the trade unions in
Germany after the World War can only result in the
workers being condemned to the rôle of the poor Lazarus,
who must be content to eat the crumbs that fall from the
rich man's table.   Collaboration is possible only where
the ends and, most important of all, the interests are the
same.

No doubt some small comforts may sometimes fall to
the share of the workers when the bourgeoisie of their
country attain some advantage over that of another
country ; but this always happens at the cost of their own
freedom and the economic oppression of other peoples.
The worker in England, France, Holland, and so on,
participates to some extent in the profits which, without
effort on their part, fall into the laps of the bourgeoisie of
his country from the unrestrained exploitation of colonial
peoples ; but sooner or later there comes the time when
those people, too, wake up, and he has to pay all the more
dearly for the small advantages he has enjoyed.   Events
in Asia will show this still more clearly in the near future.
Small gains arising from increased opportunity of employment and higher wages may accrue to the worker in a
successful state from the carving out of new markets at
the cost of others ; but at the same time their brothers
on the other side of the border have to pay for them by
unemployment and the lowering of their standard of living.
The result is an ever widening rift in the international
labour movement, which not even the loveliest resolutions
by international congresses can put out of existence.
By this rift the liberation of the workers from the yoke
of wage-slavery is pushed farther and farther into the
distance.   As long as the worker ties up his interests
with those of the bourgeoisie of his country instead of
with those of his class, he must logically also take in his

stride all the results of that relationship. He must stand ready to fight the wars of the possessing classes for the retention and extension of their markets, and to defend any injustice they may perpetrate on other peoples. The Socialist press of Germany was merely being consistent when, at the time of the World War, they urged the annexation of foreign territory. This was merely the inevitable result of the intellectual attitude and the methods which the political labour parties had pursued for a long time before the War. Only when the workers in every country shall come to understand clearly that their interests are everywhere the same, and out of this understanding learn to act together, will the effective basis be laid for the international liberation of the working class.

Every time has its peculiar problems and its own peculiar methods of solving those problems. The problem that is set for our time is that of freeing man from the curse of economic exploitation and political and social enslavement. The era of political revolutions is over, and where such still occur they do not alter in the least the bases of the capitalist social order. On the one hand it becomes constantly clearer that bourgeois democracy is so degenerate that it is no longer capable of offering effective resistance to the threat of Fascism. On the other hand political Socialism has lost itself so completely in the dry channels of bourgeois politics that it no longer has any sympathy with the genuinely Socialistic education of the masses and never rises above the advocacy of petty reforms. But the development of capitalism and the modern big state have brought us to-day to a situation where we are driving on under full sail toward a universal catastrophe. The last World War and its economic and social consequences, which are to-day constantly working more and more disastrously, and which have grown into a definite danger to the very existence of all human culture, are sinister signs of the times which no man of insight can misinterpret. It, therefore, concerns us to-day to reconstruct the economic life of the peoples from the ground up and build it up anew in the spirit of Socialism. But only the producers themselves are fitted for this task, since they are the only value-creating element in society out of which a new future can arise. Theirs must be the task of freeing labour from all the fetters which economic exploitation has fastened on it, of freeing society from all the institutions and procedure of political power, and of opening the way to an alliance of free groups of men and women based on co-operative labour and a planned administration of things in the interest of the community. To prepare the toiling masses in city and country for this great goal and to bind them together as a militant force is the objective of modern Anarcho-Syndicalism, and in this its whole purpose is exhausted.

5

THE METHODS OF ANARCHO-SYNDICALISM

Anarcho-Syndicalism and political action ; The significance of political rights ; Direct action versus parliamentarism ; The strike and its meaning for the workers ; The Sympathetic Strike ; The General Strike ; The Boycott ; Sabotage by the workers ; Sabotage by capitalism ; The Social Strike as a means of social protection ; Anti-militarism.

IT has often been charged against Anarcho-Syndicalism that it has no interest in the political structure of the different countries, and consequently no interest in the political struggles of the time, and confines its activities entirely to the fight for purely economic demands. This idea is altogether erroneous and springs either from outright ignorance or wilful distortion of the facts. It is not the political struggle as such which distinguishes the Anarcho-Syndicalists from the modern labour parties, both in principle and tactics, but the form of this struggle and the aims which it has in view. They by no means rest content with the ideal of a future. society without overlordship ; their efforts are also directed, even to-day, at restricting the activities of the state and blocking its influence in every department of social life wherever they see an opportunity. It is these tactics which mark off Anarcho-Syndicalist procedure from the aims and methods of the political labour parties, all of whose activities tend constantly to broaden the sphere of influence of the political power of the state and to extend it in ever greater measure over even the economic life of society. But by this, in the outcome, the way is merely prepared for an era of state capitalism, which according to all experience may prove to be just the opposite of what Socialism is actually striving for.

The attitude of Anarcho-Syndicalism toward the political power of the present-day state is exactly the same as it takes toward the system of capitalist exploitation. Its adherents are perfectly clear that the social injustices of that system rest, not on its unavoidable excrescences, but in the capitalist economic order as such. But, while their efforts are directed at abolishing the existing form of capitalist exploitation and replacing it by a Socialist order, they never for a moment forget to work also by every means at their command to lower the rate of profit of the capitalists under existing conditions, and to raise the producer's share of the products of his labour to the highest possible.

Anarcho-Syndicalists pursue the same tactics in their fight against that political power which finds its expression in the state. They recognize that the modern state is just the consequence of capitalist economic monopoly, and the class divisions which this has set up in society, and merely serves the purpose of maintaining this status by every oppressive instrument of political power. But, while they are convinced that along with the system of exploitation its political protective device, the state, will also disappear, to give place to the administration of public affairs on the basis of free agreement, they do not at all overlook that the efforts of the worker within the existing political order must always be directed toward defending all achieved political and social rights against

every attack of reaction, constantly widening the scope
of these rights wherever the opportunity for this presents
itself.

For just as the worker cannot be indifferent to the
economic conditions of his life in existing society, so he
cannot remain indifferent to the political structure of his
country. Both in the struggle for his daily bread and for
every kind of propaganda looking toward his social
liberation he needs political rights and liberties, and he
must fight for these himself in every situation where they
are denied him, and must defend them with all his
strength whenever the attempt is made to wrest them
from him. It is, therefore, utterly absurd to assert
that the Anarcho-Syndicalists take no interest in the
political struggles of the time. The heroic battle of the
C.N.T. in Spain against Fascism is, perhaps, the best
proof that there is not a grain of truth in this idle talk.

But the point of attack in the political struggle lies, not
in the legislative bodies, but in the people. Political
rights do not originate in parliaments, they are, rather,
forced upon parliaments from without. And even their
enactment into law has for a long time been no guarantee
of their security. Just as the employers always try to
nullify every concession they had made to labour as soon
as opportunity offered, as soon as any signs of weakness
were observable in the workers' organizations, so governments also are always inclined to restrict or to abrogate
completely rights and freedoms that have been achieved
if they imagine that the people will put up no resistance.
Even in those countries where such things as freedom
of the press, right of assembly, right of combination, and
the like, have long existed, governments are constantly
trying to restrict those rights or to reinterpret them by
judicial hair-splitting. Political rights do not exist

because they have been legally set down on a piece of paper, but only when they have become the ingrown habit of a people, and when any attempt to impair them will meet with the violent resistance of the populace. Where this is not the case, there is no help in any parliamentary Opposition or any Platonic appeals to the constitution. One compels respect from others when he knows how to defend his dignity as a human being. This is not only true in private life, it has always been the same in political life as well.

The peoples owe all the political rights and privileges which we enjoy to-day in greater or lesser measure, not to the good will of their governments, but to their own strength. Governments have employed every means that lay in their power to prevent the attainment of these rights or to render them illusory. Great mass movements among the people and whole revolutions have been necessary to wrest these rights from the ruling classes, who would never have consented to them voluntarily. One need only study the history of the past three hundred years to understand by what relentless struggles every right has had to be wrested inch by inch from the despots. What hard struggles, for example, had the workers in England, France, Spain, and other countries to endure to compel their governments to recognize the right of trade union organization. In France the prohibition against trade unions persisted until 1886. Had it not been for the incessant struggles of the workers, there would be no right of combination in the French Republic even to-day. Only after the workers had by direct action confronted parliament with accomplished facts, did the government see itself obliged to take the new situation into account and give legal sanction to the trade unions. *What is important is not that governments have decided to concede certain rights to the people, but the reason why they have had to do this.* To him who fails to understand the connection here history will always remain a book with seven seals.

Of course, if one accepts Lenin's cynical phrase and thinks of freedom as merely a " bourgeois prejudice," then, to be sure, political rights and liberties have no value at all for the workers. But then all the countless struggles of the past, all the revolts and revolutions to which we owe those rights, are also without value. To proclaim this bit of wisdom it would hardly have been necessary to overthrow tsarism, for even the censorship of Nicholas II would certainly have had no objection to the designation of freedom as a "bourgeois prejudice." Moreover, the great theorists of reaction, Joseph de Maistre and Louis Bonald, had already done this, though in different words, and the defenders of absolutism had been very grateful to them.

But the Anarcho-Sydicalists would be the very last to mistake the importance of these rights to the workers. If they, nevertheless, reject any participation in the work of bourgeois parliaments, it is not because they have no sympathy with political struggles in general, but because they are firmly convinced that parliamentary activity is for the workers the very weakest and most hopeless form of the political struggle. For the bourgeois classes the parliamentary system is without a doubt an appropriate instrument for the settlement of such conflicts as arise, and for making profitable collaboration possible, as they are all equally interested in maintaining the existing economic order and the political organization for the protection of that order. Now, where a common interest exists, a mutual agreement is possible and serviceable to all parties. But for the working class the situation is very

different. For them the existing economic order is the
source of their economic exploitation, and the organized
power of the state the instrument of their political and
social subjection. Even the freest ballot cannot do away
with the glaring contrast between the possessing and the
non-possessing classes in society. It can only serve to
impart to a system of social injustice the aspect of legal
right and to induce the slave to set the stamp of legality
on his own servitude.

But, most important of all, practical experience has
shown that the participation of the workers in parliamentary activity cripples their power of resistance and
dooms to futility their warfare against the existing system.
Parliamentary participation has not brought the workers
one iota nearer to their final goal ; it has even prevented
them from protecting the rights they have won against
the attacks of the reaction. In Prussia, for example, the
largest state in Germany, where the Social Democrats
until shortly before Hitler's accession to power were the
strongest party in the government and had control of the
most important ministries in the country, Herr von Papen,
after his appointment as Reichskanzler by Hindenburg,
could venture to violate the constitution of the land and
dissolve the Prussian ministry with only a lieutenant and
a dozen soldiers. When the Socialist Party in its help-
lessness could think of nothing do to after this open
breach of the constitution except to appeal to the high
court of the Reich instead of meeting the perpetrators of
the *coup d'etat* with open resistance, the reaction knew
that they had nothing more to fear and from then on
could offer the workers what they pleased. The fact is
that von Papen's *coup d'etat* was merely the start along
the road to the Third Reich.

Anarcho-Syndicalists, then, are not in any way opposed

to the political struggle, but in their opinion this struggle, too, must take the form of direct action, in which the instruments of economic power which the working class has at its command are the most effective. The most trivial wage-fight shows clearly that, whenever the employers find themselves in difficulties, the state steps in with the police, and even in some cases with the militia, to protect the threatened interests of the possessing classes. It would, therefore, be absurd for them to overlook the importance of the political struggle. Every event that affects the life of the community is of a political nature. In this sense every important economic action, such, for example, as a general strike, is also a political action and, moreover, one of incomparably greater importance than any parliamentary proceeding. Of a political nature is likewise the battle of the Anarcho-Syndicalists against Fascism and the anti-militarist propaganda, a battle which for decades was carried on solely by the libertarian Socialists and the Syndicalists, and which was attended by tremendous sacrifices.

The fact is that, when the Socialist labour parties have wanted to achieve some decisive political reform, they have always found that they could not do so by their own strength and have been obliged to rely wholly on the economic fighting power of the working class. The political general strikes in Belgium, Sweden and Austria for the attainment of universal suffrage are proof of this. And in Russia it was the great general strike of the working people that in 1905 pressed the pen into the tsar's hand for the signing of the constitution. What the heroic struggle of the Russian intelligenzia had not been able to accomplish in decades, the united economic action of the working class quickly brought to fulfilment.

The focal point of the political struggle lies, then, not

in the political parties, but in the economic fighting
organizations of the workers. It was the recognition
of this which impelled the Anarcho-Syndicalists to centre
all their activity on the Socialist education of the masses
and on the utilization of their economic and social power.
Their method is that of direct action in both the economic
and the political struggles of the time. That is the only
method which has been able to achieve anything at all
in every decisive moment in history. And the bourgeoisie in its struggles against absolutism has also made
abundant use of this method, and by refusal to pay taxes,
by boycott and revolution, has defiantly asserted its
position as the dominant class in society. So much the
worse if its representatives of to-day have forgotten the
story of their fathers, and howl bloody murder at the
" unlawful methods " of the workers fighting for liberation. As if the law had ever permitted a subject class to
shake off its yoke.

By direct action the Anarcho-Syndicalists mean every
method of immediate warfare by the workers against
their economic and political oppressors. Among these
the outstanding are : the strike, in all its gradations from
the simple wage-struggle to the general strike ; the
boycott ; sabotage in its countless forms ; anti-militarist
propaganda ; and in peculiarly critical cases, such, for
example, as that in Spain to-day, armed resistance of the
people for the protection of life and liberty.

Among these fighting techniques the strike, that is,
organized refusal to work, is the most used. It plays in
the industrial age the same rôle for the workers as did their
frequent uprisings for the peasants in the feudal era.
In its simplest form it is for the workers an indispensable
means of raising their standard of living or defending
their attained advantages against the concerted measures

of the employers. But the strike is for the workers not only a means for the defence of immediate economic interests, it is also a continuous schooling for their powers of resistance, showing them every day that every least right has to be won by unceasing struggle against the existing system.

Just as are the economic fighting organizations of the workers, so also are the daily wage-struggles a result of the capitalist economic order, and consequently, a vital necessity for the workers. Without these they would be submerged in the abyss of poverty. Certainly the social problem cannot be solved by wage-struggles alone, but they are the best educative instrument for making the workers acquainted with the real essence of the social problem, training them for the struggle for liberation from economic and social slavery. It may also be taken as true that so long as the worker has to sell hands and brain to an employer, he will in the long run never earn more than is required to provide the most indispensable necessities of life. But these necessities of life are not always the same, but are constantly changing with the demands which the worker makes on life.

Here we come to the general cultural significance of the labour struggle. The economic alliance of the producers not only affords them a weapon for the enforcement of better living conditions, it becomes for them a practical school, a university of experience, from which they draw instruction and enlightenment in richest measure. The practical experiences and occurrences of the everyday struggles of the workers find an intellectual precipitate in their organizations, deepen their understanding, and broaden their intellectual outlook. By the constant intellectual elaboration of their life experiences there are developed in individuals new needs and the urge for different fields of intellectual life. And precisely in this development lies the great cultural significance of those struggles.

   True intellectual culture and the demand for higher interests in life does not become possible until man has achieved a certain material standard of living, which makes him capable of these. Without this preliminary any higher intellectual aspirations are out of the question. Men who are constantly threatened by direst misery can hardly have much understanding of the higher cultural values. Only after the workers, by decades of struggle, had conquered for themselves a better standard of living could there be any talk of intellectual and cultural development among them. But it is just these aspirations of the workers which the employers view with deepest distrust. For capitalists as a class, the well-known saying of the Spanish minister, Juan Bravo Murillo, still holds good to-day: "*We need no men who can think among the workers ; what we need is beasts of toil.*"

   One of the most important results of the daily economic struggles is the development of solidarity among the workers, and this has for them a quite different meaning from the political coalition of parties whose following is composed of people of every social class. A feeling of mutual helpfulness, whose strength is constantly being renewed in the daily struggle for the necessities of life, which is constantly making the most extreme demands on the co-operation of men subjected to the same conditions, operates very differently from abstract party principles, which for the most part are of only Platonic value. It grows into the vital consciousness of a community of fate, and this gradually develops into a new sense of right, and becomes the preliminary ethical assumption of every effort at the liberation of an oppressed class.

To cherish and strengthen this natural solidarity of the workers and to give to every strike movement a more profoundly social character, is one of the most important tasks which the Anarcho-Syndicalists have set themselves. For this reason the sympathetic strike is one of their choicest weapons, and has developed in Spain to a compass it has not attained in any other country. Through it the economic battle becomes a deliberate action of the workers as a class. The sympathetic strike is the collaboration of related, but also of unrelated, categories of labour, to help the battle of a particular trade to victory by extending the strike to other branches of labour, where this is necessary. In this case the workers are not satisfied with giving financial assistance to their fighting brethren, but go further, and by crippling entire industries cause a break in the whole economic life in order to make their demands effective.

To-day, when by the formation of national and international trusts and cartels private capitalism grows more and more into monopoly capitalism, this form of warfare is in most cases the only one by which the workers can still promise themselves success. Because of the internal transformation in industrial capitalism the sympathetic strike becomes for the workers the imperative of the hour. Just as the employers in their cartels and protective organizations are building an ever broader basis for the defence of their interests, so also the workers must turn their attention to creating for themselves by an ever wider alliance of their national and international economic organizations the required basis for solidaric mass action adequate for the demands of the time. The restricted strike is to-day losing more and more of its original importance, even if it is not doomed to disappear altogether. In the modern economic struggle between

capital and labour the big strike, involving entire industries, will play a larger and larger part. Even the workers
in the old craft organizations, which are as yet untouched
by Socialist ideas, have grasped that, as is shown clearly
enough by the rapid springing up of industrial unions in
America in contrast with the old methods of the A.F. of L.

Direct action by organized labour finds its strongest
expression in the general strike, in the stoppage of work
in every branch of production by the organized resistance
of the proletariat, with all the consequences arising from
it. It is the most powerful weapon which the workers
have at their command, and gives the most comprehensive
expression to their strength as a social factor. After the
French trade union congress in Marseilles (1892), and the
later congresses of the C.G.T. (General Federation of
Labour) had by a large majority declared for the propaganda of the general strike, it was the political labour
parties in Germany and most other countries which
assailed most violently this form of proletarian action, and
rejected it as " Utopian." " The general strike is
general madness " was the trenchant phrase which was
coined at that time by one of the most prominent leaders
of the German Social Democracy. But the great
general strike movement of the years immediately following, in Spain, Belgium, Italy, Holland, Russia, and so
on, showed clearly that this alleged " Utopia " lay wholly
within the realm of the possible and did not arise merely
from the imagination of a few revolutionary fanatics.

The general strike is, of course, not an agency that can
be invoked arbitrarily on every occasion. It needs
certain social assumptions to give it its proper moral
strength and make it a proclamation of the will of the
broad masses of the people. The ridiculous claim,
which is so often attributed to the Anarcho-Syndicalists,

that it is only necessary to proclaim a general strike in order to achieve a Socialist society in a few days, is, of course, just a silly invention of evil-minded opponents bent on discrediting an idea which they cannot attack by any other means.

The general strike can serve various purposes. It can be the last stage of a sympathetic strike, as, for example, the general strike in Barcelona in February, 1902, or that in Bilbao in October, 1903, which enabled the mine-workers to get rid of the hated truck system and compelled the employers to establish sanitary conditions in the mines. It can as easily be a means by which organized labour tries to enforce some general demand, as, for example, in the attempted general strike in the U.S.A. in 1886, to compel the granting of the eight-hour day in all industries. The great general strike of the English workers in 1926 was the result of a planned attempt by the employers to lower the general standard of living of the workers by a cut in wages.

But the general strike can also have political objectives in view, as, for example, the fight of the Spanish workers in 1904, for the liberation of political prisoners, or the general strike in Catalonia in July, 1909, to compel the government to terminate the war in Morocco. And the general strike of the German workers in 1920, which was instituted after the so-called Kapp putsch and put an end to a government that had attained to power by a military uprising, belongs in this category ; as do also the mass strikes in Belgium in 1903, and in Sweden in 1909, to compel the granting of universal suffrage, and the general strike of the Russian workers in 1905, for the granting of the constitution. But in Spain the wide-spread strike movement among the workers and peasants after the Fascist revolt in July, 1936, developed into a

" social general strike " (huelga general) and led to armed
resistance, and with this to the abolishment of the capitalist
economic order and the reorganization of the economic
life by the workers themselves.

The great importance of the general strike lies in this :
At one blow it brings the whole economic system to a
standstill and shakes it to its foundations. Moreover,
such an action is in no wise dependent on the practical
preparedness of all the workers, as all the citizens of a
country have never participated in a political overturn.
That the organized workers in the most important
industries quit work is enough to cripple the entire
economic mechanism, which cannot function without the
daily provision of coal, electric power, and raw materials
of every sort. But when the ruling classes are confronted with an energetic, organized working class,
schooled in daily conflict, and are aware of what they have
at stake, they become much more willing to make the
necessary concessions, and, above all, they fear to take a
course with the workers which might drive them to
extremes. Even Jean Jaurès who, as a Socialist parlia-
mentarian, was not in agreement with the idea of the
general strike, had to concede that the constant danger
arising from the possibility of such a movement ad-
monished the possessing classes to caution, and, above
everything, made them shrink from the suppression of
hard-won rights, since they saw this could easily lead to
catastrophe.

But at the time of a universal social crisis, or when, as
to-day in Spain, the concern is to protect an entire people
against the attacks of benighted reactionaries, the general
strike is an invaluable weapon, for which there is no
substitute. By crippling the whole public life it makes
difficult mutual agreements of the representatives of the

ruling classes and the local officials with the central government, even when it does not entirely prevent them. Even the use of the army is, in such cases, directed at very different tasks from those of political revolt. In the latter case it suffices for the government, so long as it can rely on the military, to concentrate its troops in the capital and the most important points in the country, in order to meet the danger that threatens.

A general strike, however, leads inevitably to a scattering of the military forces, as in such a situation the important concern is the protection of all important centres of industry and the transport system against the rebellious workers. But this means that military discipline, which is always strongest when soldiers operate in large formations, is relaxed. Where the military in small groups faces a determined people fighting for its freedom, there always exists the possibility that at least a part of the soldiers will reach some inner insight and comprehend that, after all, it is their own parents and brothers at whom they are pointing their weapons. For militarism, also, is primarily a psychologic problem, and its disastrous influence always manifests itself most perilously where the individual is given no chance to think about his dignity as a human being, no chance to see that there are higher tasks in life than lending oneself to the uses of a bloody oppressor of one's own people.

For the workers the general strike takes the place of the barricades of the political uprising. It is for them a logical outcome of the industrial system whose victims they are to-day, and at the same time it offers them their strongest weapon in their struggle for liberation, provided they recognize their own strength and learn how to use this weapon properly. William Morris, with the prophetic vision of the poet, foresaw this development in affairs,

when, in his splendid book, *News from Nowhere,* he has
the Socialist reconstruction of society preceded by a long
series of general strikes of ever increasing violence, which
shook the old system to its deepest foundation, until at
last its supporters were no longer able to put up any
resistance against this new enlightenment of the toiling
masses in town and country.

The whole development of modern capitalism, which
is to-day growing into an ever graver danger to society,
can but serve to spread this enlightenment more widely
among the workers. The fruitlessness of the participation of the organized workers in parliaments, which is
to-day becoming more and more manifest in every
country, of itself compels them to look about for new
methods for the effective defence of their interests and
their eventual liberation from the yoke of wage-slavery.

Another important fighting device for direct action is
the boycott. It can be employed by the workers both
in their character of producers and of consumers. A
systematic refusal of consumers to buy from firms that
handle goods not produced under conditions approved
by the labour unions can often be of decisive importance,
especially for those branches of labour engaged in the
production of commodities of general use. At the same
time the boycott is very well adapted to influencing public
opinion in favour of the workers, provided it is accompanied by suitable propaganda. The union label is an
effective means of facilitating the boycott, as it gives the
purchaser the sign by which to distinguish the goods he
wants from the spurious. Even the masters of the Third
Reich experienced what a weapon the boycott can become
in the hands of great masses of people, when they had to
confess that the international boycott against German
goods had inflicted serious damage on German export

trade. And this influence might have been greater still, if the trade unions had kept public opinion alert by incessant propaganda, and had continued to foster the protest against the suppression of the German labour movement.

As producers the boycott provides the workers with the means of imposing an embargo on individual plants whose owners show themselves especially hostile to trade unions. In Barcelona, Valencia, and Cadiz the refusal of the longshoremen to unload German vessels compelled the captains of those vessels to discharge their cargoes in North African harbours. If the trade unions in other countries had resolved on the same procedure, they would have achieved incomparably greater results than by Platonic protests. In any case the boycott is one of the most effective fighting devices in the hands of the working class, and the more profoundly aware of this device the workers become, the more comprehensive and successful will they become in their everyday struggles.

Among the weapons in the Anarcho-Syndicalist armoury sabotage is the one most feared by the employer and most harshly condemned as " unlawful." In reality we are dealing here with a method of economic petty warfare that is as old as the system of exploitation and political oppression itself. It is, in some circumstances, simply forced upon the workers, when every other device fails. Sabotage consists in the workers putting every possible obstacle in the way of the ordinary modes of work. For the most part this occurs when the employers try to avail themselves of a bad economic situation or some other favourable occasion to lower the normal conditions of labour by curtailment of wages or by lengthening of the hours of labour. The term itself is derived from the French word, *sabot*, wooden shoe, and

means *to work clumsily as if by sabot blows.* The whole
import of sabotage is actually exhausted in the motto :
for bad wages, bad work. The employer himself acts
on the same principle, when he calculates the price of his
goods according to their quality. The producer finds
himself in the same position : his goods are his labour-
power, and it is only right and proper that he should try
to dispose of it on the best terms he can get.

But when the employer takes advantage of the evil
situation of the producer to force the price of his labour-
power as low as possible, he need not wonder when the
latter defends himself as well as he can and for this
purpose makes use of the means which the circumstances
put in his hand. The English workers were already
doing this long before revolutionary Syndicalism was
spoken of on the Continent. In fact the policy of
" *ca' canny* " (go slow), which, along with the phrase
itself, the English workers took over from their Scottish
brethren, was the first and most effective form of sabotage.
There are to-day in every industry a hundred means by
which the workers can seriously disturb production ;
everywhere under the modern system of division of
labour, where often the slightest disturbance in one
branch of the work can bring to a standstill the whole
process of production. Thus the railway workers in
France and Italy by the use of the so-called *grève perlée*
(string-of-pearls strike) threw the whole system of transportation into disorder. For this they needed to do
nothing more than to adhere to the strict letter of the
existing transport laws, and thus make it impossible for
any train to arrive at its destination on time. When the
employers are once faced with the fact that even in
an unfavourable situation, where the workers would not
dare to think of a strike, they still have in their hands the

means of defending themselves, there will also come to them the understanding that it does not pay to make use of some particular hard situation of the workers to force harder conditions of living upon them.

The so-called *sit down strike*, which was transplanted from Europe to America with such surprising rapidity and consists in the workers remaining in the plant day and night without turning a finger in order to prevent the installing of strike-breakers, belongs in the realm of sabotage. Very often sabotage works thus : before a strike the workers put the machines out of order to make the work of possible strike-breakers harder, or even impossible for a considerable time. In no field is there so much scope for the imagination of the worker as in this. But the sabotage of the workers is always directed against the employers, never against the consumers. In his report before the congress of the C.G.T. in Toulouse in 1897, Emile Pouget laid special stress on this point. All the reports in the bourgeois press about bakers who had baked glass in their bread, or farm hands who had poisoned milk, and the like, are malicious inventions, designed solely to prejudice the public against the workers.

Sabotaging the consumers is the age-old privilege of the employers. The deliberate adulteration of provisions, the construction of wretched slums and insanitary tene-ments of the poorest and cheapest material, the destruc-tion of great quantities of food-stuffs in order to keep up prices, while millions are perishing in direst misery, the constant efforts of the employers to force the subsistence of the workers down to the lowest level possible, in order to grab for themselves the highest possible profits, the shameless practice of the armament industries of supply-ing foreign countries with complete equipment for war, which, given the appropriate occasion, may be employed

to lay waste the country that produced them, all these
and many more are merely individual items in an inter-
minable list of types of sabotage by capitalists against
their own people.

Another effective form of direct action is the *social
strike*, which will, without doubt, in the immediate future
play a much larger part. It is concerned less with the
immediate interests of the producers than with the
protection of the community against the most pernicious
outgrowths of the present system. The social strike
seeks to force upon the employers a responsibility to the
public. Primarily it has in view the protection of the
consumers, of whom the workers themselves constitute
the great majority. The task of the trade union has
heretofore been restricted almost exclusively to the
protection of the worker as producer. As long as the
employer was observing the hours of labour agreed on
and paying the established wage this task was being
performed. In other words : *the trade union is interested
only in the conditions under which its members work, not
in the kind of work they perform.* Theoretically it is,
indeed, asserted that the relation between employer and
employee is based upon a contract for the accomplishment
of a definite purpose. The purpose in this case is social
production. But a contract has meaning only when both
parties participate equally in the purpose. In reality,
however, the worker has to-day no voice in determining
production, for this is given over completely to the
employer. The consequence is that the worker is
debased by doing a thousand things which constantly
serve only to injure the whole community for the advantage of the employer. He is compelled to make use of
inferior and often actually injurious materials in the
fabrication of his products, to erect wretched dwellings,

to put up spoiled foodstuffs, and to perpetrate innumerable acts that are planned to cheat the consumer.

To interfere vigorously here, is, in the opinion of the Anarcho-Syndicalists, the great task of the trade unions in the future. An advance in this direction would at the same time enhance the position of the workers in society, and in large measure confirm that position. Various efforts in this field have already been made, as witness, for example, the strike of the building-workers in Barcelona, who refused to use poor material and the wreckage from old buildings in the erection of workers' dwellings (1902), the strikes in various large restaurants in Paris because the kitchen workers were unwilling to prepare for serving cheap, half-decayed meat (1906), and a long list of similar instances in recent times ; all going to prove that the workers' understanding of their responsibility to society is growing. The resolution of the German armament workers at the congress in Erfurt (1919) to make no more weapons of war and to compel their employers to convert their plants to other uses, belongs also in this category. And it is a fact that this resolution was maintained for almost two years, until it was broken by the Central Trades Unions. The Anarcho-Syndicalist workers of Sömmerda resisted with great energy to the last, when their places were taken by members of the " free labour unions."

As outspoken opponents of all nationalist ambitions the revolutionary Syndicalists, especially in the Latin countries, have always devoted a very considerable part of their activity to anti-militarist propaganda, seeking to hold the workers in soldiers' coats loyal to their class and to prevent their turning their weapons against their brethren in time of a strike. This has cost them great sacrifices ; but they have never ceased their efforts, because they know that they can regain their rights only by incessant warfare against the dominant powers. At the same time, however, the anti-militarist propaganda contributes in large measure to oppose the threat of wars to come with the general strike. The Anarcho-Syndicalists know that wars are only waged in the interest of the ruling classes; they believe, therefore, that any means is justifiable that can prevent the organized murder of peoples. In this field also the workers have every means in their hands, if only they possess the desire and the moral strength to use them.

Above all it is necessary to cure the labour movement of its internal ossification and rid it of the empty sloganeering of the political parties, so that it may forge ahead intellectually and develop within itself the creative conditions which must precede the realization of Socialism. The practical attainability of this goal must become for the workers an inner certainty and must ripen into an ethical necessity. The great final goal of Socialism must emerge from all the practical daily struggles, and give them a social character. In the pettiest struggle, born of the needs of the moment, there must be mirrored the great goal of social liberation, and each such struggle must help to smooth the way and strengthen the spirit which transforms the inner longing of its bearers into will and deed.

6

THE EVOLUTION OF ANARCHO-SYNDICALISM

Revolutionary syndicalism in France and its influence on the labour movement in Europe ; The Industrial Workers of the World ; Syndicalism after the World War ; The Syndicalists and the Third International ; The founding of the new International Workingmen's Association ; Anarcho-Syndicalism in Spain ; In Portugal ; In Italy ; In France ; In Germany ; In Sweden ; In Holland ; In South America.

THE modern Anarcho-Syndicalist movement in Europe, with the single exception of Spain, where from the days of the First International Anarcho-Syndicalism has always been the dominant tendency in the labour movement, owes its origin to the rise of revolutionary Syndicalism in France, with its field of influence in the C.G.T. This movement developed quite spontaneously within the French working class as a reaction against political Socialism, the cleavages in which for a long time permitted no unified trade union movement. After the fall of the Paris Commune and the outlawing of the International in France the labour movement there had taken on an utterly colourless character and had fallen completely under the influence of the bourgeois Republican, J. Barberet, whose slogan was : " Harmony between capital and labour ! " Not until the congress in Marseilles (1879) did any Socialist tendencies again manifest themselves and the *Fédération des Travailleurs* come into being, itself to come quickly and completely under the influence of the so-called Collectivists.

But even the Collectivists did not long remain united, and the Congress of St. Etienne (1882) brought a split in this movement. One section followed the school of the Marxist, Jules Guesde, and founded the *Parti Ouvrie Français*, while the other section attached itself to the former Anarchist, Paul Brousse, to form the *Parti Ouvrier Révolutionaire Socialiste Français*. The former found its support chiefly in the *Fédération Nationale des Syndicats*, while the latter had its stronghold in the *Fédération des Bourses du Travail de France* (Federation of Labour Exchanges of France). After a short time the so-called Allemanists, under the leadership of Jean Alleman, broke away from the Broussists and attained a powerful influence in some of the large syndicates ; they had given up parliamentary activity completely. Besides these there were the Blanquists, united in the *Comité Révolutionaire Central*, and the Independent Socialists, who belonged to the *Société pour l'Economie Sociale*, which had been founded in 1885, by Benoit Malon, and out of which came both Jean Jaurès and Millerand.

All these parties, with the exception of the Allemanists, saw in the trade unions merely recruiting schools for their political objectives, and had no understanding whatever of their real functions. The constant dissension among the various Socialist factions was naturally carried over into the syndicats, with the result that when the trade unions of one faction went on strike, the syndicats of the other faction walked in on them as strike-breakers. This untenable situation gradually opened the workers' eyes, an awakening to which the anti-parliamentary propaganda of the Anarchists, who since 1883 had had a strong following among the workers in Paris and Lyons, contributed not a little. So the Trade Union Congress at Nantes (1894) charged a special committee with the task of devising ways and means for bringing about an understanding among all the trade union alliances. The result was the founding in the following year at the congress in Limoges, of the C.G.T., which declared itself independent of all political parties. It was the final renunciation by the trade unions of political Socialism, whose operations had crippled the French labour movement for years and deprived it of its most effective weapon in its fight for liberation.

From then on there existed in France only two large trade union groups, the C.G.T. and the Federation of Labour Exchanges, until in 1902, at the Congress of Montpellier the latter joined the C.N.T. With this there was brought about practical unity of the trade unions. This effort at the unification of organized labour was preceded by an intensive propaganda for the general strike, for which the congresses at Marseilles (1892), Paris (1893), and Nantes (1894) had already declared by strong majorities. The idea of the general strike was first brought into the trade union movement by the Anarchist carpenter, Tortelier, who had been deeply stirred by the general strike movement in the U.S.A. in 1886-7, and it had latter been taken up by the Allemanists, while Jules Guesde and the French Marxists had emphatically pronounced against it. However, both movements furnished the C.N.T. with a lot of its most distinguished representatives : from the Allemanists came, in particular, V. Griffuelles ; from the Anarchists, F. Pelloutier, the devoted and highly intelligent secretary of the Federation of Labour Exchanges, E. Pouget, editor of the official organ of the C.G.T., *La Voix du Peuple*, P. Delesalle, G. Yvetot, and many others. One often encounters in other countries the widely disseminated opinion, which was fostered by Werner Sombart in particular, that revolutionary Syndicalism in France owes its origin to intellectuals like G. Sorel, E. Berth, and H. Lagardelle, who in the periodical, *Le Mouvement Socialiste*, founded in 1899, elaborated in their own way the intellectual results of the new movement. This is utterly false. These men never belonged to the movement themselves, nor had they any mentionable influence on its internal development. Moreover, the C.G.T. was not composed exclusively of revolutionary trade unions ; certainly half of its members were of reformist tendency and had only joined the C.G.T. because even they recognized that the dependence of the trade unions on political parties was a misfortune for the movement. But the revolutionary wing, which had the most energetic and active elements in organized labour on its side and had at its command, moreover, the best intellectual forces in the organization, gave to the C.G.T. its characteristic stamp, and it was they, exclusively, who determined the development of the ideas of revolutionary Syndicalism.

With it the ideas of the old International wakened to new life, and there was initiated that storm-and-stress period of the French labour movement, whose revolutionary influences made themselves felt far beyond the boundaries of France. The great strike movements and the countless prosecutions of the C.G.T. by the government merely strengthened their revolutionary verve, and caused the new ideas to find their way also into Switzerland, Germany, Italy, Holland, Belgium, Bohemia, and the Scandinavian countries. In England also the

Syndicalist Education League, which had been brought
into being in 1910, by Tom Mann and Guy Bowman, and
whose teachings exercised a very strong influence,
especially among the rank-and-file of the transport and
mining industries, as was revealed in the great strike
movements of that period, owed its existence to French
Syndicalism.

The influence of French Syndicalism on the international labour movement was strengthened in great
degree by the internal crisis which at that time laid hold
of nearly all the Socialist labour parties. The battle
between the so-called Revisionists and the rigid Marxists,
and particularly the fact that their very parliamentary
activities forced the most violent opponents of revisionism
of natural necessity to travel in practice the revisionist
path, caused many of the more thoughtful element to
reflect seriously. Thus it came about that most of the
parties found themselves driven by the force of circumstances, often against their will, to make certain
concessions to the general strike idea of the Syndicalists.
Before this Domela Nieuwenhuis, the pioneer of the
Socialist labour movement in Holland, had brought up
in the International Congress of Socialists in Brussels
(1891) a proposal for warding off the approaching danger
of a war by preparing organized labour for the general
strike, a proposal which was most bitterly opposed by
Wilhelm Liebknecht in particular. But in spite of this
opposition almost all national and international Socialist
congresses were subsequently obliged to concern themselves more and more with this question.

At the Socialist congress in Paris in 1899, the future
minister, Aristide Briand, argued for the general strike
with all his fiery eloquence and succeeded in having an
appropriate resolution adopted by the congress. Even the

French Guesdists, who had previously been the bitterest
foes of the general strike, found themselves obliged
at the congress in Lille (1904) to adopt a resolution
favouring it, as they feared they would otherwise lose
all their influence with the workers. Of course nothing
was gained by such concessions. The see-saw back and
forth between parliamentarism and direct action could
only cause confusion. Straightforward men like Domela
Nieuwenhuis and his followers in Holland, and the
Allemanists in France, drew the inevitable inference from
their new conception of things and withdrew entirely
from parliamentary activity ; for the others, however,
their concessions to the idea of the general strike were
merely lip service, with no clear understanding behind it.
Whither that led was shown nicely in the case of Briand,
who, as minister, found himself in the tragic-comic
situation of being obliged to prohibit his own address in
favour of the general strike, which the C.G.T. had
distributed in pamphlet form by the hundred thousand.

Independent of European Syndicalism there developed
in the U.S.A. the movement of the *Industrial Workers
of the World*, which was wholly the outgrowth of American
conditions. Still it had in common with Syndicalism
the methods of direct action and the idea of a Socialist
reorganization of society by the industrial and agricultural
organizations of the workers themselves. As its founding
congress in Chicago (1905) the most diverse radical
elements in the American labour movement were represented : Eugene Debs, Bill Haywood, Charles Moyer,
Daniel De Leon, W. Trautmann, Mother Jones, Lucy
Parsons and many others. Its most important section
for a considerable time was the *Western Federation of
Miners*, whose name was known everywhere for its
devoted and self-sacrificing labour fights in Colorado,

Montana, and Idaho. Since the great movement for the eight-hour day in 1886-7, which came to its tragic conclusion with the execution of the Anarchists, Spies, Parsons, Fischer, Engel and Lingg, on November 11, 1887, the American labour movement had been completely bogged down spiritually. It was believed that by the founding of the I.W.W. it might be possible to put the movement back on its revolutionary course, an expectation which has thus far not been fulfilled. What chiefly distinguished the I.W.W. from the European Syndicalists was its strongly defined Marxist views, which were impressed on it more particularly by Daniel De Leon, while European Syndicalists had conspicuously adopted the Socialist ideas of the libertarian wing of the First International.

The I.W.W. had an especially strong influence on the itinerant workers in the West, but they also gained some influence among factory workers in the eastern states, and conducted a great many wide-spread strikes, which put the name of the " Wobblies " in everybody's mouth. They took an outstanding part in the embittered battles for the safeguarding of freedom of speech in the western states, and made many terrible sacrifices of life and liberty in doing so. Their members filled the jails by thousands, many were tarred and feathered by fanatical vigilantes, or lynched outright. The Everett massacre of 1916, the execution of the labour poet, Joe Hill, in 1915, the Centralia affair in 1919, and a lot of similar cases, in which defenceless workers fell victims, are only a few mile-stones in the I.W.W.'s history of sacrifice.

The outbreak of the World War affected the labour movement like a natural catastrophe of enormous scope. After the assassinations at Sarajevo, when everybody felt that Europe was driving under full sail toward a

general war, the C.G.T. proposed to the leaders of the
German trade unions that organized labour in the two
countries should take joint action to halt the threatened
disaster.   But the German labour leaders, who always
opposed any direct mass action, and in their long years
of parliamentary routine had long since lost every trace
of revolutionary initiative, could not be won over to
such a proposal.   So failed the last chance of preventing
the frightful catastrophe.

After the war the peoples faced a new situation.
Europe was bleeding from a thousand wounds and
writhing as if in the throes of a fever.   In Central Europe
the old regime had collapsed.   Russia found herself in
the midst of a social revolution of which no one could
see the end.   Of all the events after the war the occurrences
in Russia had impressed the workers in every country
most deeply.   They felt instinctively that they were in
the midst of a revolutionary situation, and that, if nothing
decisive came out of it now, all the hopes of the toiling
classes would be dispelled for years.   The workers
recognized that a system which had been unable to
prevent the horrible catastrophe of the World War,
but instead for four long years had driven the peoples to
the slaughter-pen, had forfeited its right to existence,
and they hailed any effort which promised them a way
out of the economic and political chaos which the war
had created.   For just this reason they based the highest
hopes on the Russian revolution and thought it marked
the inauguration of a new era in the history of the
European peoples.

In 1919 the Bolshevist Party, which had attained to
power in Russia, issued an appeal to all the revolutionary
workers' organizations in the world, and invited them to a
congress which was to meet in Russia in the following

year to set up a new International. Communist parties existed at that time in only a few countries ; on the other hand, there were in Spain, Portugal, Italy, France, Holland, Sweden, Germany, England, and the countries of North and South America Syndicalist organizations, some of which exercised a very strong influence. It was, therefore, of deep concern to Lenin and his followers to win these particular organizations, as he had so thoroughly alienated himself from the Socialist labour parties that he could scarcely count upon their support. So it came about that, at the congress for the founding of the Third International in the summer of 1920, almost all the Syndicalist and Anarcho-Syndicalist organizations of Europe were represented.

But the impressions which the Syndicalist delegates received in Russia were not calculated to make them regard collaboration with the Communists as either possible or desirable. The " dictatorship of the prole-tariat " was already revealing itself in its worst light. The prisons were filled with Socialists of every school, among them many Anarchists and Anarcho-Syndicalists. But above all it was plain that the new dominant caste was in no way fitted for the task of genuine Socialist reconstruction.

The foundation of the Third International, with its dictatorial apparatus of organization and its effort to make the whole labour movement in Europe into an instrument of the foreign policy of the Bolshevist state, quickly made plain to the Syndicalists that there was no place for them in that organization. But it was very necessary for the Bolshevists, and for Lenin in particular, to establish a hold on the Syndicalist organizations abroad, as their importance, especially in the Latin countries, was well known. For this reason it was

decided to set up, alongside the Third International, a
separate international alliance of all revolutionary trade
unions, in which the Syndicalist organizations of all
shades could also find a place. The Syndicalist delegates
agreed to the proposal and began negotiations with
Losovsky, the commissioner of the Communist International. But he demanded that the new organization
should be subordinate to the Third International, and that
the Syndicates in the several countries should be placed
under the leadership of the Communist organizations
in their countries. This demand was unanimously
rejected by the Syndicalist delegates. As they were
unable to come to an agreement on any terms, it was at
last decided to hold an international trade union congress
in Moscow the following year, 1921, and to leave the
decision of this question to it.

In December, 1920, an international Syndicalist
conference convened in Berlin to decide upon an attitude
toward the approaching congress in Moscow. The
conference agreed upon seven points, on the acceptance
of which their entrance into the Red Trade Union
International was made dependent. The most important
of these seven points was the complete independence
of the movement from all political parties, and insistence
on the viewpoint that the Socialist reorganization of
society could only be carried out by the economic organizations of the producing classes themselves. At the
congress in Moscow in the following year the Syndicalist
organizations were in the minority. The *Central Alliance
of Russian Trade Unions* dominated the entire situation
and put through all the resolutions.

In conjunction with the thirteenth congress of the
F.A.U.D. (*Freie Arbeiter-Union Deutschlands*, Free
Labour Union of Germany), at Düsseldorf in October,

1921, there was held an international conference of Syndicalist organizations, at which delegates from Germany, Sweden, Holland, Czechoslovakia, and the I.W.W. in America were present. The conference voted for the calling of an international Syndicalist congress in the spring of 1922. Berlin was selected as the meeting place. In July, 1922, a conference was held in Berlin to make preparations for this congress ; France, Germany, Norway, Sweden, Holland, Spain, and the revolutionary Syndicalists in Russia were represented. The Central Alliance of Russian Trade Unions had also sent a delegate, who did his best to prevent the calling of the congress, and when he had no success in this left the conference. The conference worked out a declaration of the principles of revolutionary Syndicalism, which was to be laid before the coming congress for consideration, and made all the necessary preparations for making the congress a success.

The International Congress of Syndicalists met in Berlin from December 25, 1922, until January 2, 1923, the following organizations being represented : Argentina by the *Federación Obrera Regional Argentina*, with 200,000 members ; Chile by the *Industrial Workers of the World*, with 20,000 members ; Denmark by the *Union for Syndicalist Propaganda*, with 600 members ; Germany by the *Freie Arbeiter-Union*, with 120,000 members ; Holland by the *National Arbeids Sekretariat*, with 22,500 members ; Italy by the *Unione Sindicale Italiana*, 500,000 members ; Mexico by the *Confederación General de Trabajadores*, with 30,000 members ; Norway by the *Norsk Syndikalistik Federasjon*, with 20,000 members ; Portugal by the *Confederaçao Geral do Trabalho*, with 150,000 members ; Sweden by the *Sveriges Arbetares Centralorganisation*, with 32,000 members. The Spanish C.N.T. was at that time engaged

in a terrific struggle against the dictatorship of Primo de
Rivera, and for that reason had sent no delegate, but they
reaffirmed their adherence at the secret congress in
Saragossa in October, 1923. In France, where after the
war a split in the C.G.T. had taken place, leading to the
founding of the C.G.T.U., the latter had already joined
the Muscovites. But there was a minority in the organization which had combined to form the *Comité de Défense
Syndicaliste Revolutionaire*. This committee, which
represented about 100,000 workers, took active part in
the proceedings of the Berlin congress. From Paris the
Fédération du Batiment with 32,000 members and the
Fédération des Jeunesses de la Seine were likewise represented. Two delegates represented the Syndicalist
minority of the Russian trade unions.

The congress resolved unanimously on the founding
of an international alliance of all Syndicalist organizations
under the name *International Workingmen's Association*.
It adopted the declaration of principles that had been
worked out by the Berlin preliminary conference, which
presented an outspoken profession of Anarcho-Syndicalism. The second item in this declaration runs as
follows :

" Revolutionary Syndicalism is the confirmed enemy
of every form of economic and social monopoly, and
aims at its abolition by means of economic communes
and administrative organs of field and factory workers
on the basis of a free system of councils, entirely
liberated from subordination to any government or
political party. Against the politics of the State and
of parties it erects the economic organization of labour ;
against the government of men, it sets up the management of things. Consequently, it has for its object,
not the conquest of political power, but the abolition

of every State function in social life. It considers that, along with the monopoly of property, should disappear also the monopoly of domination, and that any form of the State, including the dictatorship of the proletariat, will always be the creator of new monopolies and new privileges ; it could never be an instrument of liberation."

With this the breach with Bolshevism and its adherents in the separate countries was completed. The I.W.M.A. from then on travelled its own road and gained a footing in a number of countries which had not been represented at the founding congress. It holds its international congresses, issues its bulletins, and adjusts the relations between the Syndicalist organizations of the different countries. Among all the international alliances of organized labour it is the one that has most faithfully cherished the traditions of the First International.

The most powerful and influential organization in the I.W.M.A. is the Spanish C.N.T., which is making history in Europe to-day and is, moreover, discharging one of the hardest tasks that has ever been set before a workers organization. The C.N.T. was founded in 1910, and within a few years counted as members over a million workers and peasants. The organization was new only in name, not in objectives or methods. The history of the Spanish labour movement is shot through with long periods of reaction, in which the movement has been able to carry on only an underground existence. But after every such period it has organized anew. The name changes, but the goal remains the same. The labour movement in Spain goes back to 1840, when the weaver, Juan Munts, in Catalonia, brought into being in Barcelona the first trade union of textile workers. The government of that day sent General Zapatero to Catalonia to put

down the movement. The consequence was the great
general strike of 1855, which led to an open revolt in which
the workers inscribed on their banners the slogan :
Asociación ó Muerte ! (The right to organize or death !)
The rebellion was bloodily suppressed, but the movement
continued underground until, later, the government
granted the workers the right of organization.

This first movement of the Spanish workers was
strongly influenced by the ideas of Pi y Margall, leader of
the Spanish Federalists and disciple of Proudhon. Pi
y Margall was one of the outstanding thinkers of his time
and had a powerful influence on the development of
libertarian ideas in Spain. His political ideas had much
in common with those of Richard Price, Joseph Priestley,
Thomas Paine, Jefferson, and other representatives of the
Anglo-American liberalism of the first period. He wanted
to limit the power of the state to a minimum and gradually
replace it by a Socialist economic order. In 1868, after
the abdication of King Amadeo I, Bakunin addressed his
celebrated manifesto to the Spanish workers, and sent a
special delegation to Spain to win the workers to the First
International. Tens of thousands of workers joined the
great workers' alliance and adopted the Anarcho-
Socialists ideas of Bakunin, to which they have remained
loyal to this day. As a matter of fact, the Spanish
Federation was the strongest organization in the International. After the overthrow of the first Spanish republic
the International was suppressed in Spain, but it continued to exist as an underground movement, issued its
periodicals, and bade defiance to every tyranny. And
when, finally, after seven years of unheard-of persecution,
the exceptional law against the workers was repealed,
there immediately sprang to life the *Federacion de
Trabajadores de la Región Española*, at whose second

congress in Sevilla (1882) there were already represented 218 local federations with 70,000 members.

No other workers' organization in the world has had to endure such frightful persecution as the Anarchist labour movement in Spain. Hundreds of its adherents were executed or horribly tortured by inhuman inquisitors in the prisons of Jerez de la Frontera, Montjuich, Sevilla, Alcalá del Valle, and so on. The bloody prosecutions of the so-called *Mano Negra* (Black Hand), which actually never existed, and was a pure invention of the agents of the government to justify the suppression of the organizations of the field workers in Andalusia ; the gruesome tragedy of Montjuich, which in its day roused a storm of protest from the entire world ; the acts of terrorism of the *Camisas Blancas* (White Shirts), a gangster organization which had been brought into existence by the police and the employers to clear away the leaders of the movement by assassination, and to which even the General Secretary of the C.N.T., Salvador Segui, fell victim—these are just a few chapters in the long, torture-filled story of the Spanish labour movement. Francisco Ferrer, founder of the Modern School in Barcelona and publisher of the paper, *La Huelga General* (The General Strike), was one of its martyrs. But no reaction was ever able to crush the resistance of its adherents. That movement has produced hundreds of the most marvellous characters, whose purity of heart and inflexible idealism had to be acknowledged even by their grimmest opponents. The Spanish Anarchist labour movement had no place for political careerists. What it had to offer was constant danger, imprisonment, and often death. Only when one has become acquainted with the frightful story of the martyrs of this movement does one understand why it has assumed at certain

periods such a violent character in defence of its human
rights against the onslaughts of black reactionaries.

The present C.N.T.-F.A.I. embodies the old traditions
of the movement. In contrast with the Anarchists of
many other countries, their comrades in Spain from the
beginning based their activities on the economic fighting
organizations of the workers. The C.N.T. to-day
embraces a membership of two and a half million workers
and peasants. It controls thirty-six daily papers, among
them *Solidaredad Obrera* in Barcelona, with a circulation
of 240,000, the largest of any paper in Spain, and *Castilla
Libre*, which is the most read paper in Madrid. Besides
these the movements put out a lot of weekly publications
and possesses six of the best reviews in the country.
During the last year, in particular, it has published a
large number of excellent books and pamphlets and has
contributed more to the education of the masses than has
any other movement. The C.N.T.-F.A.I. is, to-day,
the backbone of the heroic battle against Fascism in
Spain and the soul of the social reorganization of the
country.

In Portugal, where the labour movement has always
been strongly influenced by neighbouring Spain, there
was formed in 1911 the *Confederaçao Geral do Trabalho*,
the strongest workers' organization in the country,
representing the same principles as the C.N.T. in Spain.
It has always sharply stressed its independence of all
political parties, and has conducted a lot of big strike
movements. By the victory of the dictatorship in
Portugal the C.G.T. was forced out of public activity and
to-day leads an underground existence. The recent
disturbances in Portugal, directed against the existing
reaction, are chiefly traceable to its activities.

In Italy there always existed, from the days of the

First International, a strong Anarchist movement which, in certain sections of the country retained a decisive influence over the workers and peasants. In 1902 the Socialist Party founded the *Confederazione del Lavoro*, which was patterned after the model of the German trade unions and had for its purpose the affiliation of all the trade union organizations of the country. But it never attained this goal ; it was not even able to prevent a large part of its membership from being strongly influenced by the ideas of the French Syndicalists. A few big and successful strikes, especially the farm-labourers' strike in Parma and Ferrara, gave a strong impetus to the prestige of the advocates of direct action. In 1912 there convened in Modena a conference of various organizations which were not at all in accord with the methods of the Confederation and its subservience to the influence of the Socialist Party. This conference formed a new organization under the name, *Unione Sindicale Italiana*. This body was the soul of a long list of severe labour struggles up to the outbreak of the World War. In particular it took a prominent part in the occurrences of the so-called *Red Week* in June, 1913. The brutal attacks of the police on striking workers in Ancona led to general strike, which in a few provinces developed into an armed insurrection.

When, in the following year, the World War broke out, a serious crisis arose in the U.S.I. The most influential leader of the movement, Alceste de Ambris, who had all the time played a rather ambiguous rôle, tried to rouse in the organization a sentiment for the war. At the congress in Parma (1914), however, he found himself in the minority and, with his followers, withdrew from the movement. Upon Italy's entrance into the war all the known propagandists of the U.S.I. were arrested and imprisoned until the end of the war. After the war a revolutionary situation developed in Italy, and the events in Russia, whose actual significance could at that time, of course, not be foreseen, roused a vigorous response in the country. The U.S.I. in a short time awoke to new life and soon counted 600,000 members. A series of serious labour disturbances shook the country, reaching their peak in the occupation of the factories in August, 1920. Its goal at that time was a free soviet system, which was to reject any dictatorship and find its basis in the economic organizations of organized labour.

In that same year the U.S.I. sent its secretary, Armando Borghi, to Moscow to acquaint himself personally with the situation in Russia. Borghi returned to Italy sadly disillusioned. In the interim the Communists had been trying to get the U.S.I. into their hands ; but the congress at Rome in 1922 led to an open break with Bolshevism and the affiliation of the organization with the I.W.M.A. Meanwhile Fascism had developed into an immediate danger. A strong and united labour movement that was determined to risk everything in defence of its freedom could still have put a check upon this danger. But the pitiful conduct of the Socialist Party and the Confederation of Labour, which was subject to its influence, wrecked everything. Besides the U.S.I. there remained only the *Unione Anarchica Italiana* to rally round the universally revered champion of Italian Anarchism, Errico Malatesta. When in 1922 the general strike against Fascism broke out, the democratic government armed the Fascist hordes and throttled this last attempt at the defence of freedom and right. But Italian democracy had dug its own grave. It thought it could use Mussolini as a tool against the workers, but it thus became its own grave-digger. With the victory of

Fascism the whole Italian labour movement disappeared, and along with it the U.S.I. and all openness in social life.

In France after the war the so-called reformist wing had gained the upper hand in the C.G.T., whereupon the revolutionary elements seceded and formed themselves into the C.G.T.U. But, since Moscow had a very strong interest in getting this particular organization into its hands, there was started in it an unscrupulous underground activity in cells after the Russian pattern, which went so far that in 1922 two Anarcho-Syndicalists were shot down by Communists in the Paris Trade Union house. Thereupon the Anarcho-Syndicalists, with Pierre Benard, withdrew from the C.G.T.U., and formed the *Confédération Générale du Travail Syndicaliste Révolutionaire*, which joined the International Workingmen's Association. This organization has since then been vigorously active and has contributed greatly to keep alive among the workers the old pre-war ideas of the C.G.T. The disillusionment over Russia and, above all, the resounding echo among the French workers of the Spanish fight for freedom, led to a strong revival of revolutionary Syndicalism in France, so that one can safely count on a rebirth of the movement within predictable time.

In Germany there had existed for a long time before the war the movement of the so-called *Localists*, whose stronghold was the *Freie Vereinigung deutscher Gewerkschaften*, founded by G. Kessler and F. Kater in 1897. This organization was originally inspired by purely Social Democratic ideas, but it combated the centralizing tendencies of the general German trade union movement. The revival of revolutionary Syndicalism in France had a strong influence on this movement, and this was notably strengthened when the former Social Democrat and later

Anarchist, Dr. R. Friedeberg, came out for the general
strike. In 1908 the F.V.D.G. broke completely with
Social Democracy and openly professed Syndicalism.
After the war this movement took a sharp upswing and
in a short time counted 120,000 members. At its
congress in Berlin in 1919 the declaration of principles
worked out by R. Rocker was adopted; this was in
essential agreement with the objectives of the Spanish
C.N.T. At the congress in Düsseldorf (1920), the organization changed its name to *Freie Arbeiter-Union Deutschlands*. The movement carried on an unusually active
propaganda and took an especially energetic part in the
great actions by organized labour in the Rhenish
industrial field. The F.A.U.D. rendered a great service
through the tireless labours of its active publishing-house,
which, in addition to a voluminous pamphlet literature,
brought out a large number of longer works by Kropotkin,
Bakunin, Nettlau, Rocker and others, and by this activity
spread the libertarian ideas of these men to wider circles.
The movement, in addition to its weekly organ, *Der
Syndikalist*, and the theoretical monthly, *Die Internationale*, had at its command a number of local sheets,
among them the daily paper, *Die Schöpfung*, in Düsseldorf. After Hitler's accession to power the movement
of the German Anarcho-Syndicalists vanished from the
scene. A great many of its supporters languished in
concentration camps or had to take refuge abroad. In
spite of this the organization still exists in secret, and
under most difficult conditions carries on its underground propaganda.

In Sweden there has existed for a long time a very active
Syndicalist movement, the *Sveriges Arbetares Central-
organization*, which is also affiliated with the I.W.M.A.
This organization numbers over 40,000 members, which

constitutes a very high percentage of the Swedish labour movement. The internal organization of the Swedish Syndicalists is in very excellent condition. The movement has two daily papers, one of them, *Arbetaren*, managed by Albert Jensen in Stockholm. It has at its disposal a large number of distinguished propagandists, and has also inaugurated a very active Syndicalist Youth movement. The Swedish Syndicalists take a strong interest in all the workers' struggles in the country. When, on the occasion of the great strike of Adalen, the Swedish government for the first time sent militia against the workers, five men being shot down in the affray, and the Swedish organized workers replied with a general strike, the Syndicalists played a prominent part, and the government was at last compelled to make concessions to the protest movement of the workers.

In Holland as Syndicalist movement there was the *Nationale Arbeeter-Sekretariat* (N.A.S.), which counted 40,000 members. But when this came steadily more and more under Communist influence, the *Nederlandisch Syndikalistisch Vakverbond* split off from it and announced its affiliation with the I.W.M.A. The most important unit in this new organization is the metal workers' union under the leadership of A. Rousseau. The movement has carried on, especially in recent years, a very active propaganda, and possesses in *De Syndikalist*, edited by Albert De Jong, an excellent organ. And the monthly *Grond-Slagen*, which appeared for a few years under the editorship of A. Müller-Lehning, deserves also to be mentioned here. Holland has been from of old the classic land of anti-militarism. Domela Nieuwenhuis, former priest and later Anarchist, highly respected by everyone for his pure idealism, in 1904 founded the *Anti-Militarist International*, which, however, had influence worth

mentioning only in Holland and France. At the third
anti-militarist congress at The Hague (1921) the International *Anti-Militarist Bureau against War and Reaction*
was founded, which for the past sixteen years has carried
on an extremely active international propaganda, and has
found able and unselfish representatives in men like
B. de Ligt and Albert de Jong. The Bureau was represented at a number of international peace congresses and
put out a special press-service in several languages.
In 1925 it allied itself with the I.W.M.A. through the
International Anti-military Committee, and in association
with that organization carries on a tireless struggle against
reaction and the peril of new wars.

In addition to these there exist Anarcho-Syndicalist
propagandist groups in Norway, Poland, and Bulgaria,
which are affiliated with the I.W.M.A. Likewise the
Japanese *Jiyu Rengo Dantai Zenkoku Kaigi* had entered
into formal alliance with the I.W.M.A.

In South America, especially in Argentina, the most
advanced country on the southern continent, the young
labour movement was from the very beginning strongly
influenced by the libertarian ideas of Spanish Anarchism.
In 1890 to Buenos Aires from Barcelona came Pellicer
Parairo, who had lived through the time of the First
International and was one of the champions of libertarian
Socialism in Spain. Under his influence a congress of
trade unions convened in Buenos Aires in 1891, from
which arose the *Federación Obrera Argentina*, which at
its fourth congress changed its name to *Federación Obrera
Regional Argentina*. The F.O.R.A. has carried on since
then without interruption, even though its efficiency was
often, as it is again to-day, disturbed by periods of reaction, and it was driven to underground activity. It
is an Anarchist trade union organization, and it was the

soul of all the great labour struggles which have so often shaken that country. The F.O.R.A. began its activity with 40,000 members, which number has grown since the World War to 300,000. Its history, which A. D. de Santillan has sketched in his work, " F.O.R.A.," is one of the most battle-filled chapters in the annals of the international labour movement. For over twenty-five years the movement had a daily paper, *La Protesta*, which under the editorship of Santillan and Arango, for years published a weekly supplement to which the best minds of international libertarian Socialism contributed. The paper was suppressed after the *coup d'etat* of General Uribura, but it continues to appear in an underground edition even to-day, even if not quite daily. Moreover, almost every considerable trade union had its own organ. The F.O.R.A. early joined the I.W.M.A., having been represented at its founding congress by two delegates.

In May, 1929, the F.O.R.A. summoned a congress of all the South American countries, to meet in Buenos Aires. To it the I.W.M.A. sent from Berlin its Corresponding Secretary, A. Souchy. At this congress, besides the F.O.R.A. of Argentina, there were represented : Paraguay by the *Centro Obrero del Paraguay ;* Bolivia by the *Federación Local de la Paz, La Antorcha,* and *Luz y Libertad ;* Mexico by the *Confederación General de Trabajadores ;* Guatemala by the *Comité pro Acción Sindical ;* Uruguay by the *Federación Regional Uruguaya.* From Brazil trade unions from seven of the constituent states were represented, Costa Rica was represented by the organization, *Hacia la Libertad.* Even the Chilean I.W.W. sent representatives, although since the dictatorship of Ibanez it had been able to carry on only underground activities. At this congress the *Continental American Workingmen's Association* was brought into

existence, constituting the American division of the
I.W.M.A. The seat of this organization was at first in
Buenos Aires, but later, because of the dictatorship, it
had to be transferred to Uruguay.

These are the forces which Anarcho-Syndicalism at
present has at its disposal in the several countries.
Everywhere it has to carry on a difficult struggle against
reaction as well as against the conservative elements in
the present labour movement. Through the heroic
battle of the Spanish workers the attention of the world
is to-day directed to this movement, and its adherents
are firmly convinced that a great and successful future
lies before them.

BIBLIOGRAPHY

Adamic Louis. *Dynamite.* The Story of Class Violence in America, 1931.
Baginski, Max. *Syndicalismus ;* Lebendige, keine toten Gewerkschaften, 1925.
Bakunin, Michael. *God and the State*, 1895.
   Michael Bakunins Gesammelte Werke, 3 vols., 1923-25.
Beer, Max. *Social Struggles and Modern Socialism*, 1926.
Berkman, Alexander. *Prison Memoirs of an Anarchist*, 1912.
   The Bolshevik Myth, 1925.
   The Anti-Climax, 1925.
   Now and after. ABC of Communist Anarchism, 1929.
Besnard, Pierre. *Les syndicats ouvriers et la révolution sociale.*
   Le monde nouveau.
   Anarcho-Syndicalisme et les anarchistes, 1937.
Brissenden, P. F. *The I.W.W. :* A Study of American Syndicalism, 1919.
Brupbacher, Fritz. *Marx und Bakunin*, 1913.
Cleyre, Voltairine de. *Selected Works*, 1914.
Cole, G. D. H. *Social Theory*, 1920.
   Workshop Organization, 1923.
   Organized Labour, 1924.
   Robert Owen, 1925.
Cook, A. J. *The Nine Days*, 1926.
Cornelissen, Ch. *Ueber den internationalen Syndikalismus*, 1910.

Craik, W. W. *A Short History of the Modern British Working Class Movement*, 1919.

Dashar, M. *The Revolutionary Movement in Spain*, 1934.

David, H. *The History of the Haymarket Affair*, 1936.

Delesalle, P. *Les deux méthodes du syndicalisme*, 1907.
L'action syndicaliste et les anarchistes, 1900.

De Ligt, B. *La paix créatrice*, 1935.

Domela-Nieuwenhuis, F. *Socialism in Danger*, 1895.

Eltzbacher, Paul. *Anarchism*, 1908.

Foster, W. M. Z. & Earl C. Ford. *Syndicalism*.

Godwin, William. *Political Justice*, 1793.

Goldman, Emma. *Anarchism and other Essays*, 1911.
My Disillusionment in Russia, 1923.
Living my Life, 1931.

Griffelhes, V. *L'action syndicaliste*, 1908.

Guillaume, James. *L'Internationale, documents et souvenirs*, 4 vols. 1905-10.

Haywood, W. *Bill Haywood's Book*, 1929.

Hunter, Robert. *Violence and the Labour Movement*, 1914.

I.A.M.B. *War Against War*, 1925.

I.W.M.A. *Zehn Jahre internationaler Klassenkampf*, 1932.

Kropotkin, Peter. *Anarchist Communism*; its basis and principles, 1891.
The Conquest of Bread, 1892.
The State : its Role in History, 1898.
Fields, Factories and Workshops, 1899.
Memoirs of a Revolutionist, 1899.
Modern Science and Anarchism, 1900.
Mutual Aid : A Factor of Evolution, 1902.
The Modern State, 1912.
Ethics : Origin and Development, 1924.

Lagardelle, H. *La grève générale et le socialisme*, 1905.
   Le socialisme ouvrier, 1911.
Levine, L. *The Labour Movement in France*, 1912.
Louis, P. *Histoire du mouvement syndical en France*, 1907.
Malatesta, Errico. *Anarchy*, 1892.
Mann, Tom. *Prepare for Action*, 1910.
   All Hail! Industrial Solidarity! 1910.
   Symposium on Syndicalism, 1910.
Maximov, G. *Bolshevism : Promises and Reality*, 1935.
Morris, William. *News from Nowhere*, 1891.
Müller-Lehning, A. *Die Sozialdemokratie und der Krieg*, 1924.
Nearing, Scott. *The British General Strike*, 1926.
Nettlau, Max. *Responsibility and Solidarity in the Labour Struggle*, 1900.
   Errico Malatesta : The Biography of an Anarchist, 1924.
   Der Vorfrühling der Anarchie, 1925.
   Der Anarchismus von Proudhon zu Kropotkin, 1927.
   Élisée Reclus : Anarchist und Gelehrter, 1927.
   Anarchisten und Sozialrevolutionäre, 1931.
Oerter, Fritz. *Was wollen die Syndikalisten?* 1923.
Pataud and Pouget. *Syndicalism and the Co-operative Commonwealth*, 1913.
Peloutier, F. *L'organisation corporative et l'anarchie*, 1896.
   Histoire des Bourses du Travail, 1902.
Pierrot, M. *Syndicalisme et révolution*, 1908.
Postgate, R. W. *A Short History of the British Workers*, 1926.
Pouget, Emile. *The Basis of Trade Unionism*, 1910.
   La Confédération du Travail, 1908.
   Sabotage. Introduction by A. Giovannitti, 1912.
   Le Parti du Travail.

Proudhon, P. J.   *What is Property?*   1885.
   General Idea of the Revolution in the Nineteenth Century, 1923.
   De la capacité politique des classes ouvrières, 1865.
Reclus, Elisée.   *An Anarchist on Anarchy*, 1894.
   Evolution and Revolution, 1892.
   L'homme et la terre, 6 vols.   1905-08.
Rocker, Rudolf.   *Die Prinzipien des Syndikalismus*, 1920.
   Der Bankerott des russischen Staatskommunismus, 1921.
   Der Kampf ums tägliche Brot, 1925.
   The Truth about Spain, 1936.
   Nationalism and Culture, 1937.
   The Tragedy of Spain, 1937.
Roller, Arnold.   *The Social General Strike*, 1902.
   Die direkte Aktion als revolutionäre Gewerkschaftstaktik, 1906.
Russell, Bertrand.   *Roads to Freedom*, 1920.
Shapiro, A.   *The International Workingmen's Association : its Aims, its principles*, 1933.
Souchy, August.   *Spain*, 1937.
Symes, L. and Clement, T.   *Rebel America*, 1934.
Tobler, M.   *Der revolutionäre Syndikalismus*, 1922.
Trautmann, W. E.   *Handbook of Industrial Unionism*.
   Direct Action and Sabotage, 1912.
Tcherkesoff, W.   *Pages of Socialist History*, 1902.
Webb, Beatrice and Sidney.   *History of Trade Unionism*.
Yvetot, G.   *ABC syndicaliste*, 1908.
   Manuel du soldat.

Epilogue
RUDOLF ROCKER

This book was published nine years ago, when the Civil War in Spain had already reached its last phase. The defeat of the heroic Spanish workers and peasants after two years and a half of civil strife by the combined forces of Fascism destroyed the last hope for stemming the flood of reaction in Europe. Spain became the nemesis for the labour movement in Europe in general and for libertarian Socialism in particular. The Spanish people had to carry on their valiant fight for liberty, human dignity and social justice almost single-handed, while the whole world passively watched the unequal struggle. The so-called democracies of the West denied the Spaniards the materials so urgently needed in their titanic battle against their relentless foe, and organised labour in Europe and America, demoralised and split up in hostile factions, remained indifferent or helpless, when everything in Europe was at stake. They had to pay dearly for their passivity, for with Spain in the hands of Franco and his Falange the way was cleared for the Second World War and its terrible results. Even Mr Sumner Wells, the former Secretary of State of the United States, had to admit that the policy of his country towards Spain in those years of decision was one of the greatest errors America ever committed.

As for the labour movement, Franco's victory paved the way to the worst debacle the workers of Europe ever had to suffer. Under the heel of Hitler's armies, the whole labour movement in Germany, France, Italy, Poland, Czechoslovakia, Holland, Belgium, Norway and the countries in the South-East of Europe crumbled to dust, and the entire continent was turned into a desert of ruins, starvation and unspeakable misery. Even now, when two years have already passed since the end of the great slaughter, large parts of Europe are still a wilderness. Her economic life is paralysed, her means of production, her natural resources of raw materials are exhausted, and her industries and agriculture completely disorganised. That such a horrible catastrophe could not pass without leaving a deep impression upon the people in every country is self-evident. In many countries people became demoralised and apathetic as a consequence of their horrible sufferings, especially in Germany and Austria, where little hope for a speedy reconstruction of their economic and social life prevails. Nevertheless there are signs almost everywhere of an awakening and the development of new ideas to deal with the present situation.

The only way out of the present chaos, the only possibility for rebuilding the devastated countries, would be a federated Europe with a unified economy resting upon new foundations, in which no people would be isolated by artificial barriers and placed under the guardianship of hostile and stronger neighbours. This would also be the first step for a world federation with equal rights for every people, including the so-called colonial peoples, who have hitherto been the victims of foreign imperialism and hampered in their natural development. It is likewise the only means to achieve further changes and improvements within the general organism of our social life and to overcome the economic exploitation and political suppression of individuals and peoples. After the terrible experiences of the past, there is in fact no other way to accomplish a new relationship among the peoples and to prepare a new form of society and a rebirth of humanity.

In Europe such a transformation is long overdue, but its greatest obstacle is still the power policy of the larger states and their unceasing struggle for the hegemony of the continent, the eternal source of wars and the real cause why until this day one generation has always had to build up what its predecessors have destroyed.

As for Anarcho-Syndicalism and the libertarian movement in general, it is now in a state of reorganisation. With the exception of Sweden, libertarian organisations, in almost every country of Europe, have been ruthlessly suppressed during the days of the Nazi occupation and could function only as small underground groups of resistance. Sweden was one of the few countries in Europe spared by the war, and where the libertarian movement could hold its ground. When Hitler came into power in Germany the Bureau of the International Working Men's Association [IWMA], after a short interval in Holland, was transferred to Stockholm and kept alive by the syndicalist movement in Sweden. But its activity was paralysed as a result of the terrible catastrophe on the continent. The only reason for its continued existence was to prepare for the time when the war would come to an end and steps could be taken to reorganise the movement in the various countries. The Bureau in Stockholm published during all those years its *Bulletin* and tried to keep up connections wherever it was possible, but that was all that could be expected.

Of all the regional sections of the IWMA the powerful CNT in Spain has suffered most. About a million human lives were lost during the Civil War, among them many thousands of the most courageous and devoted members of the CNT and FAI. Thousands were buried alive in the dungeons and concentration camps of Franco, many of them perishing under the iron heel of their relentless torturers. And many thousands are still living in exile, waiting impatiently for their hour of return. Large numbers of the former members of the CNT are living in France, Belgium, England, North Africa, Mexico and the various countries of South America. In France thousands of these refugees have taken an active part in the underground movements against the German invasion. In all these countries our Spanish comrades in exile have created organisations of their own and are publishing papers, books and pamphlets.

In Spain itself a very active underground movement is carried on by the followers of the CNT, the FAI and the Libertarian Youth against the military dictatorship of Franco. They have their own papers printed in secret plants and are in constant touch with their comrades abroad. In some parts of Spain a kind of guerrilla warfare is still going on, especially in the mountains of Asturias where the terrain is favourable for such actions.

Among the Spanish comrades abroad there is a great deal of interesting and sometimes very ardent discussion in progress on the reorganisation of the movement after the fall of the Franco regime. The experiences of the Spanish Revolution, the war and its aftermath have created quite a number of new problems which cannot be ignored, but their real solution can only be found when the present dictatorship is overthrown and the libertarian movement in Spain reorganised. There is no doubt that our movement, which is so deeply rooted in the Spanish people, will again play an important role in the future of that country, but it is also clear that its success will be largely determined by developments in the rest of Europe.

In Germany, where every section of organised labour has been completely destroyed by the Nazis and their large property in buildings, printing plants, libraries and money confiscated, the Anarcho-Syndicalist movement had to undergo terrible ordeals. After its general office in Berlin had been raided and destroyed by the brown gangsters, the comrades in Erfurt tried to organise an underground movement, but after a short time many of the militants fell into the hands of the Nazis and landed in prisons and concentration camps. Nevertheless, underground activities were carried on in almost every part of the country, but the sacrifices were terrific. According to the reports received since connections with Germany have been re-established, about 1,200 comrades were sentenced during Hitler's regime to from five to twenty years of hard labour; about twenty were executed or died in the torture chambers of the Gestapo, and dozens perished miserably in the concentration camps. But this list is by no means complete and mainly concerns the fate of our comrades in the present American, English and French zones of Germany, while exact data for the Russian-occupied zone are not obtainable at present.

A reorganisation of the movement under the present circumstances in Germany is very difficult. One of the greatest obstacles is the division of the country into different zones and the present military administrations, which until now have only permitted the organisation of the larger political parties and the general trade union movement. Most of the German comrades believe that a reorganisation of the movement on the foundations of the old Freie Arbeiter-Union (Free Labour Union) is impossible, since in view of the devastation of the country and the hardships of the people the old methods have become meaningless. They feel that every effort has to be turned towards constructive work in rebuilding the country and lessening the present misery. Many of our comrades are already working in this direction within the newly founded trades unions, co-operative societies and other organisations where they have a possibility to spread their ideas. In the Western zones preparations have already been made for the creation of a new libertarian movement for constructive activity on a broader basis more suitable to the present conditions than the FAUD which was founded under very different circumstances.

Also in Holland, where many of our comrades took part in the underground movement during the time of the German invasion, the former members of the Nederlands Syndicalistisch Vakverbond came to the conclusion that by reviving the movement in its old forms they could hardly meet the new problems created by the war and the present situation in Europe. They therefore established a new federation, the Nederlandse Bond van Vrije Socialisten, whose principles are propagated in their new organ *Socialisme van onder op* (Socialism From Below), one of the most interesting periodicals of our present movement towards which many of the best-known exponents of libertarian socialism in Holland and abroad are contributing. The new movement is very active in spreading its ideas in the general trades unions and is also carrying on a courageous struggle for the independence of Indonesia and the other Dutch colonies. Besides the new federation, which has propaganda groups in every province of Holland, there are in existence a number of other organisations of libertarian character with their own papers and ways of propaganda.

In France the old members of the Confédération Générale du Travail Syndicaliste Révolutionnaire reorganised their movement soon after the end of the war. Finding it impossible to work together within the general labour movement of the CGT, which today is completely dominated by the Communist Party and has become merely an instrument for the foreign policy of the Russian dictatorship, they tried to rally their old adherents and to form a new movement. They held their first convention as early as December 1946 in Paris, where delegates of the Spanish CNT and a representative of the IWMA also were present. The name of the organisation was changed into Confédération Nationale du Travail (CNT), and its activity based upon the same *Declaration of Principles* advocated by the IWMA before the war. Their organ is *L'Action Syndicaliste.*

Besides this movement of the Anarcho-Syndicalists in France, most of the libertarian groups are organised in the Fédération Anarchiste with its organ *Le Libertaire* in Paris. Since the end of the war there is a strong revival of the old libertarian movement in all parts of France which finds its representation in about seven or eight papers and magazines.

In Italy, the first country in Europe which succumbed to the yoke of Fascism, a new revival of the libertarian movement took place after the war. Most of its organisations belong to the new Federazione Anarchista Italiana, which has its headquarters in

Carrara, the centre of the Italian marble industry. The federation possesses about fifteen periodicals all over Italy and is carrying on a vivacious propaganda among the workers and peasants. Its main strongholds are Milan and Genoa. As in France, our comrades in Italy are not only combating the remnants of the still powerful Fascist and monarchist reaction, but also the growing influence of the Communist Party, which controls not only the whole trade union movement but also the larger part of the Socialist Party and is aiming for the establishment of a new dictatorship and the transformation of the country into a satellite of Russia. Here, as in most other countries of Europe, the terrible misery of the people provides one of the greatest obstacles to any progressive movement and at the same time exposes the country to the dangers of a new totalitarian reaction.

In Portugal the Confederação General de Trabalho, which has been suppressed under the dictatorship of Salazar, is still compelled to carry on an underground existence. In spite of the continual persecutions, they managed to bring out their organ *A Batalha* and other clandestine publications. Many of the militants of the CGT perished in the concentration camps of the islands of Cape Verde under conditions which can only be compared with the torture chambers of the Gestapo in Germany.

There are also libertarian groups in England, Belgium, Norway, Poland and Switzerland which are publishing periodicals, books and pamphlets and are spreading their ideas among the people. Only in the Russian-dominated countries in the South-East of Europe every attempt to create a libertarian movement has been suppressed by ruthless dictatorships, as in the case of the Bulgarian Anarcho-Syndicalists, of whom many became victims of the great blood purges in that country.

In general the libertarian movement in most countries of Europe is still in a state of reorganisation. Many of our old comrades in every country died during the war or became victims of the terrible persecutions of Fascist reaction. Under the present deplorable economic and social conditions in Europe, the task of our comrades is not an easy one, but there are nevertheless many indications that we shall soon witness another revival of the libertarian forces all over the continent.

In Latin America a great upsurge of libertarian socialism is noticeable in almost every country since the end of the war, mainly in Argentina. After a long period of clandestine existence the Federación Obrera Regional Argentina is carrying on an extensive propaganda for a six hours' labour day in every part of the country. The recent strike of the workers in the great port of Buenos Aires which ended with a great success was directed by the FORA and gained the organisation a large measure of sympathy among the workers and students. The new movement of the youth in the universities is strongly influenced by libertarian ideas and is very active.

Besides the syndicalist activity of the FORA there are many libertarian groups all over the country, publishing quite a number of anarchist periodicals and pamphlets and carrying on a vigorous propaganda in the field of education and public enlightenment. To the publishing houses Iman and especially Americale in Buenos Aires goes the credit of printing during recent years the largest number of libertarian classics and many other important works ever to be published in that country. Their editions are excellent and find a large circulation among the workers and intellectuals.

There is also a good deal of libertarian activity in most of the other countries of South and Central America, with periodicals coming out in Uruguay, Paraguay, Peru, Chile, Brazil, Colombia, Guatemala, Costa Rica, Mexico and Cuba.

In the United States, with the exception of two small monthlies, all the other libertarian publications are printed in Spanish, Italian, Yiddish and Russian. There is no organised movement on national lines in this country to match those found in Europe, but there are quite a number of associations of various kinds and for different purposes where libertarian ideas and aspirations can be found and are appreciated. In Asia modern libertarian ideas were known in China, Japan, and among smaller circles of Indonesian students who became influenced by the libertarian movement in Holland. In Japan the small anarchist movement was completely destroyed after the execution of D. Kotoku and his comrades in January 1911. In later years an Anarcho-Syndicalist movement, the Jiyu Rengo Danetai Zenkoku Kaigi, developed in Tokyo, Nagasaki, Hiroshima and other centres of Japanese industry, which held connections with the Bureau of the IWMA in Berlin. But also this movement became soon a victim of the ruthless persecutions of the Japanese government.

In China anarchist groups existed before the war in various

towns, which published libertarian periodicals and pamphlets and kept in touch with their comrades in America and Europe. A revival of this movement took place after the war, inspired by groups of intellectuals in various places of the country.

Libertarian ideas have also recently penetrated into India, where a group of Indian intellectuals in Bombay, founders of the Indian Institute of Sociology and its organ the *Indian Sociologist*, are very active in spreading the new ideas. They also created a centre for libertarian publications, the Libertarian Book House in Bombay, which has already brought out a large number of books and pamphlets of all kinds by well-known libertarian writers in Europe and America.

The present renaissance of the libertarian movement throughout the world is the best proof that the great ideas of liberty and social justice are still alive after the horrible ordeal most countries have had to undergo, and that they are regarded as guiding principles by many intent on solving the varied new problems of our time and creating the paths for a better future and a higher level of humanity.

It is the only movement which not only carries on the fight against the many evils of present society but also tries to prevent the dangers of dictatorship of every form and shape, futile state capitalism and political totalitarianism, which can only lead to the worst slavery mankind has ever experienced.

Rudolf Rocker
Crompond, NY, June 1947

Printed and bound by CPI Group (UK) Ltd, Croydon, CR0 4YY

09/06/2025

14685865-0005